Bright with Invisible History

Praise for the writing of William Bauer

"… a poet who can get his wild sense of humour into poems that are linguistically subtle and open in form. Bauer cares about language, and loves it. The comedy is his way of exploring the large questions of life as process rather than stasis. *The Terrible Word* is both damn good and damn entertaining."
Douglas Barbour, *The Dalhousie Review*

"A gentleman—rather than a vulgarian—satirist, Bauer does not often find vice in his fellow man, but perhaps that is so because the people in his poems are liable to be more confused than destructive…. But laughter almost always wins out over despair."
Michael Brian Oliver, *The Fiddlehead*

"*A Terrible Word* has a vigour and wry humour reminiscent of Mark Twain. In 'What I Shudda Said to the Lady Who Asked Me,' Bauer's excitement is so infectious that you want to jump up on the desk beside him and shout your reply. Poems like 'Municipal Water' and 'Landscape as Tune' serve as calmer, meditative ground for the more outspoken pieces."
Cathleen Hoskins

"One of Bauer's chief strengths in *A Family Album* is a strikingly inventive imagination. We are urged to share his delight in life's absurdities, even while recognizing that the foibles he describes in others are too frequently our own."
Roger MacDonald, *Canadian Book Review Annual*

"In one of Bauer's stories, a photo of two smiling girls has caught one of them with her hands clenched in a fist. A nephew wonders, but as he says, he wonders out of love and all those who wonder for any other reason are 'voyeurs.' Bauer too wonders out of love, and his insights don't allow either himself or his readers to stoop to becoming voyeurs. He preserves and protects while missing nothing. Such tact and dignity are welcome."
Alexandra McHugh, *The Gazette* (Montreal)

"These stories are specific in capturing a recognizable region: the slow-paced, tradition-bound Eastern Seaboard. It is an idyllic world from certain angles and in certain seasons, but change the perspective, come two steps closer, and it darkens into a place betrayed and deserted by time…. For those interested in the art of narration, these stories are a pleasure to read. One savours the rich and varied vocabulary, and the experimentation with language and structure."
Carrie MacMillan, *Quill and Quire*

"*Unsnarling String* combines humour and down-to-earth philosophy, commonplace experience and delightful eccentricities. Bauer writes about simple things in life that become ridiculously tangled, and about how people reduce life's complications to simple formulas for survival…. Poems to be read aloud to family and friends."
Richard Lemm, *The Atlantic Provinces Book Review*

William Bauer, 1985

Bright with Invisible History

A William Bauer Reader

Edited by Brian Bartlett

Chapel Street Editions

Published by Chapel Street Editions
150 Chapel Street
Woodstock, NB E7M 1H4
www.chapelstreeteditions.com
chapelstreeteditons@gmail.com

ISBN: 978-1-988299-34-1

Library and Archives Canada Cataloguing in Publication
Title: Bright with invisible history : a William Bauer reader/edited by Brian Bartlett.
Other titles: Works. Selections
Names: Bauer, William, 1932-2010, author. | Bartlett, Brian, 1953- editor.
Description: Poetry, short stories, essays, book reviews, and journal entries.
Identifiers: Canadiana 20200410113 | ISBN 9781988299341 (softcover)
Classification: LCC PS8553.A84 A6 2020 | DDC C811/.54—dc23

Cover painting by William Bauer courtesy of Stephen May

Frontispiece photo of author by Brian Bartlett

Book design by Brendan Helmuth

Chapel Street Editions, Ltd. gratefully acknowledges the financial support of the
Department of Tourism, Heritage, and Culture, Province of New Brunswick.

Contents

II. Short Stories

Uncollected

Whorls, Bowlines and Sheepshanks:
Remembering William Bauer

"Because individuals differ and because from time to time human beings do listen to one another," wrote Ernest Hart Jr. in a 1970 issue of *The Fiddlehead*, "because one's language is always abuilding…honest poetic deeds are still from time to time committed." Hart's tongue-in-cheek essay on "the poem-prose" was a good-natured critique of over-florid examples of the better-known prose-poem, and a mock commentary reminiscent of those by Poe, Twain and Leacock. *Fiddlehead* readers across and beyond Canada might've wondered about the identity of Hart Jr., but the journal's editors knew him as a mask playfully worn by William Bauer, a native of Maine, a University of New Brunswick professor, and a poet who had begun publishing in their pages two years earlier. Bauer's first *Fiddlehead* appearances had been a group of poems soon included in his chapbook *Cornet Music for Plupy Shute* (New Brunswick Chapbooks, 1968) and an inventive, idiosyncratic piece of fiction called "Pig-of-the-Wind: A Fragment from the Archives." Early on, the spirit of Bauer's writings was suggested in the *Fiddlehead* piece on poem-proses; he insists on how "individuals differ," shows faith in listening and in language "abuilding," and combines casual understatement with unmistakable energy in the very syntax of his sentences.

Born in Portland, Maine in 1932, William Alfred Bauer was the son of Alfred Bauer, a first-generation American with German ancestry; and Virginia (Reardon) Bauer, whose Yankee lineage went back several generations, with earlier roots in Ireland. Alfred was a well-respected hardware-store proprietor. Before arriving in Fredericton in 1965 with his wife, Nancy (Luke) Bauer, and the first two of their three children, William completed a B.A. in Psychology from Amherst College (Massachusetts), an M.A. from Wesleyan University (Connecticut), and the course work and exams for a Ph.D. at the University of North Carolina, a degree completed in 1970 with a reputedly gargantuan dissertation, *The Letter Device in the Early English Essay Journal*. At one point Bauer also did a fiction workshop with the great Irish short-story writer Frank O'Connor. Massachusetts-born Nancy received a B.A. at Mount Holyoke, and eventually developed a strong interest in religious and philosophical writers such as Boethius, Viktor Shklovsky, William Ernest Hocking and Flannery O'Connor; she went on to publish five novels, short stories and arts journalism. The Bauers were part of an invigorating, internationalized time when Americans hired to teach in Fredericton (William's contemporaries also from the States and later destined to work for *The Fiddlehead* included Kent Thompson, Robert Cockburn and Ted Colson) worked shoulder to shoulder with other *Fiddlehead* editors such as Maritime-born Robert Gibbs, Roger Ploude and Robert Hawkes, and overseas-born Peter Thomas, Michael Taylor and James Woodfield. For many of his years on campus Bauer played various roles for *The Fiddlehead*. From 1971 to 1984 he read thousands of manuscripts as Poetry Co-Editor, Assistant Poetry Editor, Poetry Editor and Fiction Co-Editor. Three years after his 1968 chapbook, he published a second with New Brunswick Chapbooks (a series started and overseen by Nancy), *Everett Coogler*, followed by two full-length collections from Fiddlehead Poetry books, *The Terrible Word* and *Unsnarling String*, along with a collection of short stories, *A Family Album* (from Oberon Press in Ottawa).

At UNB, Bauer taught a wide variety of courses, including *Shakespeare*, *Poets of Our Time*, *American Prose and Poetry*, *Literature of Atlantic Canada*, and the advanced courses *Augustan Prose*, *The Scriblerians*, *Restoration and 18th-century Biography and Autobiography* and *Creative Writing*. My most memorable undergrad course was Bauer's Honours Seminar *18th-Century Non-fiction Prose*, a gateway into Addison and Steele, Johnson and Boswell, Defoe and Swift. Bauer's excitement with the minds and language of such writers was an opening for some of us into the values of writing that doesn't occupy the conventional genres of poetry, fiction or drama. In a journal entry written during that course, in early 1975, I copied out a few comments by Bill that I'd netted during one class, admiring and amused by their freshness: "…those watery-spined characters that keep flobbing their way across history"; "Justinian as a kind of original stage-door Johnnie"; "Genghis Khan and all those hard-riding types out of the north"; "That may be dabbling in people's fatuousness—but I love dabbling in people's fatuousness. After all, that's what the imagination is"; and, in giving us advice for writing our essays: "I hope you can talk about this in some way other than a frenzied search for metaphors for the ineffable"; "It should be something other than, 'I measured the pyramids—and then I went home.'"

During the 1970s and '80s Bill criss-crossed his beloved adopted province by car, giving dozens of readings from his poetry and fiction in schools all over New Brunswick—from Grand Falls, Bathurst and Newcastle to Harvey, Hampton and St. Stephen—as well as in Fort Kent, Presque Isle and Orono in his home state of Maine. Nancy meanwhile created, organized and taught for the annual summertime Maritime Writers' Workshop. The first audience for most of Bill's and Nancy's writing was a workshop of generous openness and great longevity: McCord Hall, a.k.a. The Ice House or Tuesday Night, an informal gathering that included student writers, several other *Fiddlehead* editors, and writers from the community. One of Bill's most striking creations was Everett Coogler, an independent vegetable-and-fruit salesman. Bill's full-bodied readings of his poems became locally legendary. They were also appreciated by poets elsewhere in the country, including Peter Anson, who chose nine of the Coogler poems for this 1969 anthology *Canada First: New Canadian Poets* (House of Anansi), and Douglas Barbour and Stephen Scobie, in whose *The Maple Laugh Forever* (Hurtig, 1981) three of Bauer's poems appeared. Audiences laughed boisterously hearing the agonies of Everett, who begins each day "brother to brother / To the Anti-Everett Cooglers / Unrolling their awnings / And opening stands / On the ass-end / Side of the moon." Everett feels harassed from all sides, by customers mistrusting his scales, policemen pilfering his cherries, his "no-good" son-in-law, and rumours that he talks to his produce. More than a colourful eccentric, Everett represents the defensiveness, fragility, pride and stubbornness most of us possess to some degree. When I heard and read the endings of two Everett poems — "It can give you / One terrible wallop" and "what is unsaid / Remains / Nifty" — the words *wallop* and *nifty* resonated with me as never before. Decades later, whenever I encounter those two words Bill's use of them often comes to mind.

The Bauers' first child, Ernie, would later honour Bill in his obituary as "a respected professor, mentor, poet and original thinker." *Original thinker*, indeed. William Bauer was the first educator I knew who often used the words "complex" and "complexity" with a savouring tone. How appropriate that his ten-part poem "Unsnarling String" (cited several times by the minister at his funeral) obsessively works through variations on metaphors of "massive / unimaginable ramified / major whorls" and of "a thousand buried grannies / bowlines and sheepshanks." The narrator of a Bauer postcard-story set in Japan is chastised by the ghost of Carl Sandburg: "You like all the subtlety and nuance in the art, and I was charmed too, but after a while piled up nuance is like a cartload of pig dung" — yet Bill was drawn to the packed, nuance-filled prose of writers like Doctor Johnson, Thoreau, both Henry and William James, Faulkner, Updike and Amado. He also championed the imagination manifested in uncelebrated, little-known places. When universities began to fill with discussions about Post-Modernism and its broadening the boundaries of "literature," Bill once said to me, "I don't get what all the fuss is about — I never believed in a 'canon' to begin with" (he once joked about having tried to get through his PhD without ever reading *King Lear*—though he would later teach Shakespeare courses). Surely Bill's recognition of creativity in multifarious forms helped make him a less single-minded writer than some; in his later decades, he spent potential writing-time on pursuits such as painting, photography, rug-hooking, jewelry-making, papier-maché art, gourd-growing-and-decorating, and, through the final dozen years of his life, a massive bibliography and gazetteer of books from and about Maine. Books and reading remained of paramount importance. The Bauer archives include a scrap of paper on which Bill wrote: "Like so many of my contemporary colleagues I trace my origins from highly literate but uneducated people who benefited immeasurably from free and accessible sources of knowledge; and the withering of libraries on behalf of expensive and closed systems of bureaucratized information fills me with acute anguish. Nothing is on my mind more than the fate of the yearning autodidact of the twenty-first century."

Bill's poetry and stories are filled with highly original characters and narrators: a window-dresser confused as a mannequin; a paranoid convinced that his private parts are displayed on a flag; "The only dependable yellow bus driver / On the only paradise route" to a cloudy afterlife; and the young Wilbur and Orville Wright, who dig up a dead horse and take it to the race-course to challenge the cliché "never bet on a dead horse." Bill published long poems or poem sequences centred on a truant officer, a barber named Herbert Barber, and Twelvebelly the Ogre. Lyrical beauties can be found in such poems as "Landscape as Tune," "Woods" and "Painting by the Numbers." Wit, pathos and affection nourish fictions like "This Story Ends in a Pinegrove," "What Is Interred with Their Bones" and "Fern" (one of the best dog stories you'll find anywhere, also very much a story about storytelling). Though Bill was no stranger to darkness, fear and danger (from a book review: "these like all times are perilous"), he once suggested in another review that humour more than either tragedy or satire was his guiding light.

Bill's responses to new books remain with us as more than ephemera. Besides giving careful, critical yet never high-handed readings of the book at hand, the reviews often made generalizing comments that remain solid years after their publication: "It is pompous to call this collection a letter to the world; pomposity should be thrown away and letters not"; "On the map, the state of Maine appears to obtrude shamelessly into Canada, wedging its way between Quebec and New Brunswick — at best a geographical nuisance, at worst looking like a protuberance of manifest destiny that has lost its sense of direction." His reviews gathered in this selection of his works have never before been reprinted. Much more personal yet equally valuable are the excerpts chosen from a journal Bill wrote for six weeks in early 1984. While he emerges in those pages as a man happy in solitude with books, music and art projects, his grounding in and love for his family — Nancy and their children Ernest, Grace and John — were unmistakable. As Ernie Bauer wrote in his father's obituary: "He created a vibrant, intimate family culture of colour, story-telling and laughter. His brilliant sense of humour turned many family suppers to hysterics…. He was a champion of the pleasures of life that one creates humbly for oneself, and he disdained high seriousness. Yet: he cared so much — for his wife, his children and his grandchildren — he worried about us, he paced when we were gone, we never thought for a minute that we were anything but the most important thing in his life."

One of several ways in which William Bauer was a rare man was in his combination of sometimes wildly fantastic, inventive poetry and prose, and the satisfactions and joys he found in daily life with those he loved. The scope of his exuberant work and play deserves an omnibus like *Bright with Invisible History*. He entertains, challenges and moves us. We should be grateful for writing that offers us so much of the gloriously snarled and unsnarled strings of both language and human lives.

Brian Bartlett

I. Poems 1968–1978

From *Cornet Music for Plupy Shute*

It Keeps on Happening

Hear now the loose-linked rocketing of wind
Unfleecing all the house that is not pinned
To house with monkeydunk and well-struck nails.
The winter purge has brought his heft of gales
And left a trail of unused parts across
A country wide with woods, at no one's loss.

In this unpeopled country I can find
On summer walks in any depth of mind
Stuck in the flesh of trees or blown against
The briars of meadow-edge now long unfenced
Dismembered weathercocks and paper tiles —
Familiar junk of mine now strewn for miles.

When winds define my figments with a blast
Unhinging, who knows how, what must be cast
Aloft as flimsy artifice unstuck
From the chinked hulk I have to call my luck,
I'm at a loss to know just what has gone
But like to find a relic later on.

Chihuahua on the Highway Going West

Sunset
Fouls the green with red
Along the middle lane
Where he with nut-sized brain
And whirling legs
Ticks away the inches and the miles
As if his course were set by stars
An endless journey to the west
Between the speeding cars.

I see
Him for a moment up ahead,
Now here, and now behind.
His purpose fills my vacant mind;
An heroic quest,
I say, for his ancestral home.
I feel with him his sparrow bones
Grow warm at last beneath the sun,
Ablaze on naked stones.

Trembling
In that oven, roasted red
With knotted joy
He fawns before a native boy
He must not hate,
And yaps forever at the stinking goats.
Happy and hairless, with his tiny lust
For being cursed and cuffed
He breathes the golden dust.

Sunset
Now has spent its red
Many miles behind,
And golden dust has left my mind
Devoid of trust
That ever stars or miles were mine
To spend along the right-hand lane
On an idle trip into a West
That now has lost its stain.

If I Don't Tell You, No One Else Will; or, How Lucky You Are To Have Your Whole Lives Before You

All out for the Cloud Forest, gang.
Last stop.
All out.
Then I turn around this old yellow bus
And go back for another load.
But before you go let me say a word
Or two,
Just a few
Remarks as a last goodby—
Some things you may not have heard.

This is the Cloud Forest, pals,
Mostly vines
And air,
And infinite spaces to swing and fall—
Catch as catch can they say
When they try to tell you
What I'm trying to tell you
What it's like in there.
It's the land of Lampwick, man,
Grade twenty-one,
Forever and never;
And no one swinging the vines in the air
Will give a hang
How it is with you,
Or blow your nose—
No mommies or daddies to tickle to death
With your personal jungles
Of matted hair—
Everything free
In the dark night air.

And the first night out
You will probably sleep
In the crotch of a tangly tree,
Fall out
And down
And catch something else on the
Easy float down
In another verdurous layer.

This is the Cloud Forest, men;
The bottom's a far piece down.
Keep swinging,
Little pals and
With luck in this land of Lampwick
Even without any clinging tails
You can hold out a claw
From time to time
And avoid the ultimate fall.

For the ultimate fall
To the Cloud Forest floor
Is a myth we no longer believe;
No catch!
With minimum scratch
In the palpable, infinite, spacious
(Oh bliss in this dark night to be alive!)
Sinuous, horny, ass-over-teakettle,
Sometimes up-falling thatch,
You may anytime offer your
Fur-padded paw and gently
And firmly once more,
Always a little bit just before,
Get taken in.

This is the Cloud Forest, gang.
All out.
Last stop.
Then I will go in my old yellow bus

All alone for another load;
Rumble down
Back to town
On the mountainous, hardscrabble road,
Get shaken again till my assbone is sore
Back over the same old route.
Low pay,
Little thanks,
Back again.
More and more, more and more —
There is always another recruit.
It's a hard, tough life, little pals,
To be
Like me
The only dependable yellow bus driver
On the only paradise route.

Old Dog Wrecks

Good old dog Wrecks
The Vth,
Who pulled how many of us youngsters
Out of waterholes and left
Us to be alive today to mourn him,
Now is dead.
We never loved him quite enough
We say,
Remembering how he always knew
The strangers in the yard
And which ones he should bite.
Old ragged-eared Wrecks—
His trouble was
He wasn't Wrecks the very Ist.
Even his smell we used to say wasn't his own
But something we made sure was bred
From bloodlines back to when
The family never even used to name
Much less to number dogs.
His lineage was like a polished
Handmedown; we had done it by ourselves
And with our wits.
Though strangely gloomy, he was good,
But why shouldn't he have been
Since he who saved us was
The product of our brains
And foresight.
The saviour of us all, old gloomy Wrecks
The guardian of the home and hearth
We thought and made.

From *Everett Coogler*

And foremost
The glorious strangers
With their sensitive eyes
Their gliding gait
And their sonorous mouths

Novalis

... and his ditch is the very mound of his meditations.

John Earle

Illustration from the cover of *Everett Coogler*
by Marjory Donaldson.

The Lament of Everett Coogler

After
17 years at
The same stand,
I,
Everett Coogler,
Would say,
That life is a stream rushing on,
Alive with
Red
Herrings.

Everett Coogler as an Emblem
of Cosmic Brotherhood

The Everett Coogler who every morning
Unrolls his awning
And opens his stand
And is ready for business
And whatever the day will bring
Stands shoulder to shoulder
And brother to brother
To the Anti-Everett Cooglers
Unrolling their awnings
And opening stands
On the ass-end
Side of the moon.

Everett Coogler Takes a Survey

"There are all kinds,
You know,
That come to my stand
In the course of a year,"
Said Everett Coogler
Hoping we'd ask him
To tell us
A little more.
"Yes sir,
There's apples
          and peaches
          and carrots
          and grapes
And pumpkins
And turnips
And squash."

Everett Coogler Agonistes

In those dear, dead days
Not quite beyond recall
When we went down to Josie's house
On Sunday afternoons,
Then old Ev Coogler used
To play first base
For the Hamsterville Fats—
Oh never, oh never again;
There are sights that a man
Can't two times see
And live.
Now Everett Coogler,
This is what he says,
Sitting beside a pile
Of his funny vegetables
Out on Highway 43,
And he means it, too,
To the degree that I would not
If I had said it.
Everett Coogler says,
Daggering a pumpkin
With his wooly eyes,
"For me, you know, for
23 years come spring,
The moon and the stars
And all the firmament,
So to speak,
Have been my
Horsehide,
And over and over I
Hit it out of the park
Because I can't run
Too fast."

Everett Coogler Takes His Stand

Take me to your bosom
O Hamsterville,
And so you damn well should
And buy my questionable vegetables —
All the way out
On Highway 43,
Past the high-toned
Dog and cat hospital
You built with the money
From Mary-Ellen's will.
You can't tell me it's useless vanity
That keeps me from
Trucking your streets
And calling about
Like the hawkers of old,
"Questionable vegetables!
Questionable vegetables!"
You don't really expect
Old Everett Coogler
To do
That.

Everett Coogler Rebukes His Wife

"Oh, Everett, come see
There is hair out here
Growing all over
The pumpkins,"
A breathless Mary-Ellen Coogler said,
One time
Long ago
When Everett and she were young.
"You have said enough,
Mary-Ellen,"
Said he.
"I've known that for years
And you'll never learn,
Or will you,
Woman,
Not to talk about things
Beyond your
Ken.
I soon found out when I opened my
Stand
That what is unsaid
Remains
Nifty."

Everett Coogler Lays Plans for a Retort

"There is a lot of sitting
At times in my business,"
Said Everett Coogler
Who was sitting at the time
When he said what he said
About sitting.
"And much of the time
I spend the time thinking
What it is I will say
To anyone who opens
His yap
With something like this:
'I don't know about them scales,
Everett,
They don't look any too reliable
To me.'"

Everett Coogler Turns Back Rumors

I am well aware of
What they always say
About me behind my back.
See if I'm not right;
They say something like this,
"That crazy old fool
Talks to the vegetables
Just like they were
People."
I'm here to tell you
That's a lie
And not even a very good one
At that.
Why all these years
I've stood firm
According to the saying that
My father said and I say too,
"It don't pay to
Be familiar
With the
Hired help."

Everett Coogler Counts and Thinks

If you count all the years
That I have been out here
At my stand on Highway 43
And think of each year
How many vegetables and fruits
And seeds
And soft drinks in the cooler
And paper bags and strings
And copies of the *Hamsterville Blade*
In a pile out front
Weighted down with a
Different vegetable every day,
And customers
And days when there aren't any,
Though everyone but customers are
Always there
In foul weather and fair,
You have yourself
An idea of what I like to think
Is the fullness of
Time and space
And event
And objects of love and hate
And even indifference.
So hairy or not
The stars and the moons
Are more than numberless;
They are completely and perfectly
Infinite.
Now when you start thinking like that,
Which you would always do well to do,
It can give you
One terrible wallop.

The Testimony of Josie's No-Good Husband

When Josie's no-good husband
Got hit by a Plymouth
As he was walking along one night
Out on Highway 43,
And had, some say,
An inconsiderate and persistent will
To live and so pulled through,
Afterwards he used to tell his
No-good, honky-tonk friends
In down-town Hamsterville
About the delusions he had
When he was close to death.
They were about Everett and his stand.
"You know," he would say
For the thirty-fifth time
While the floozies and cake-eaters
Looked painfully aside
For the thirty-fourth time
And shifted their bottoms on the stools,
"You know, there would be her old man
Sitting like a goddam idol
In his daffy stand,
Festooned with flypaper
And his arms flung over some
Pumpkins, all palsy-like,
And looking at me with his wooly eyes.
But here is the part I can't get out
Of my mind.
I knew, I knew, I knew,
That the weird old bastard
Had both of his hands on the handle
The only goddam handle
Of the whole cosmic
Works."

Two Ways of Looking at the Hamsterville Fats

There are some who might think
That the Hamsterville Fats,
For all of their class and
Thunderous power
And wing-footed speed
Made glorious now by
The generous gifts of time
Which looks at such things
Through wooly and wanting eyes,
Are worth little more than
An annual condescending story about
The old-timers in the sports page
Of the *Hamsterille Blade.*
But some there are who
Know in the night spent long and well
With blue whiskey and watermelon pie,
That washes down the bitterness
Of webby doubts and botherations
Of the honky-tonk now,
That the Hamsterville Fats
In all of the years when they were
Never lost a single game.
To hell with hairy pumpkins
Or the nodding lapses in the
Nowadays
Hamsterville,
Ailing Josie,
Bottle throwing,
Awning tearing,
Dog and cat damn it,
Waterblooded sun.
There is somewhere a storing up
And treasuring home

Amid the Godhead
For such perfections —
Such unprecedented and
Finely-grained,
Fully-juiced,
Excellence of
Youth.

Modern Fame as She Is Known in Hamsterville

Everett Coogler knows
As well as anyone in Hamsterville
The blessing and the curse
Of journalistic dignity
And decent neighbourly restraint
From the time the
Hooligans attacked his stand
Out on Highway 43
On Hallowe'en a year or two ago.
They tore away his awning,
Smashed the pumpkins
He had stacked in perfect pyramids
Out front,
And littered the Tarmac
With billions of shards
Of shattered non-returnables.
In reporting the incident,
The *Hamsterville Blade*
Gave no notice that the victim of
This unspeakable vandalism
Had still as his most
Notable achievement and worthy
Claim to immortality,
A life-time batting average of
1000% in a full career
Of playing ball for the Hamsterville Fats.
He had what few men ever have,
A record saying he had
Retired unretired.
But if this modern cub
Reporting to the *Blade*
Neglected immortality,
He also kindly

Failed to say in
Cold eternal print
What everyone in Hamsterville
Knew about the incident—
That Everett
Roused from sleep among
His filthy quilts
And unsaleable produce
Inside the stand
Had chased the bastards
A half-mile down the highway
In the dead of night,
Shrieking like a ghost indeed,
"Aphids!
Aphids!
Aphids!"

From *The Terrible Word*

The Terrible Word

The most terrible word I know
I could not bring myself to say
Or write it here on the page

It would leap to your attention
Like a turd on a white linen tablecloth

Roll around and shout at you
Until you forgot everything else
About me and my poem that is decent

For my pains
I would be forever known
As the man who put it into print
Besides I have no ambition to be called
An enemy of mankind
Or to achieve permanent notoriety at such a cost

Don't ask me what it is
I would not even whisper it
In anybody's ear much less in yours

No it is not to be found in the Bible
And it refers to no bodily function
Wholesome or perverse

It is immeasurably more bad
Than either of those things

Even in these enlightened times
I could possibly be sent to the
Electric chair for saying it

Because no one has ever been caught at it up to now
And there is no precedent yet in law
For committing such an offense

So far as I know it has only been used once
In the history of the world
In the summer of 1956
When a wholesale grocer somewhere in New Brunswick
Or maybe it was Maine
Barked his shins on the corner of
A frozen food locker

It is a God damned wonderful word

I will not tell what it is

I am saving this word

What I Shudda Said to the Lady Who Asked Me, "Shouldn't a Poet Create Beauty?"

Yes, Yes, Omigod, Yes!
Oh Jesus, Yes! Ogod, what else?
Rape the English dictionary from "a" to "zymurgy"
To do it if you have to,
Learn Romanian, Esperanto, Morse Code,
Blow whistles that only dogs can hear,
Lave the hands with scented soap and
Get a manicure to wigwag to the
Deaf and dumb, cock
Your ear on a lonely hillside
For a decade waiting to hear the
Music of the spheres and get it
Down in your head,
Talk back to the many-colored polished pebbles
Rolling and clicking in the streambeds
Of this lovely province,
Eavesdrop on thrashing lovers
In their heats,
Take a Famous Writer's Correspondence Course,
Blow all the little gleaming golden trumpets
There are in your soul and write down
Only the sweetest sweetest music
Of it and let the rest go by.

O lady, O beautiful lady,
Asking such a beautiful question
In this little room in a big building
Whirling along
And returning here every twenty-four hours
While I fill my lungs with tobacco smoke,
And the filaments in the electric lights
Over us crickle their way surely to darkness—

The fact of the matter is
I can't
There must be some terrible poison
In my system and I
Can't.

Angels

If I mean angels
Why don't I dare to say angels
And let anyone laugh who wants to
People are always laughing at angels
What with their feathers and white robes
So why should I care
When angels themselves don't mind
"To Hell with them," they say

But these angels lived in our breadbox
A polished metal one
Inside and out
And when I let down the great door
Hinged at the bottom
I could look in and see them there
Their forms mirrored on all
The inner walls of that windowless garage
It was illumined by angel light
When I shut the door again
And flipped the bakelite latch

"But that was just bread," you protest
To Hell with you as well I say
I know bread from angels any day of the week
Though I can see why you say
What you thought I thought
Risen white shapes towering there
The blurry images on all sides

I wet my finger with my tongue
And ran it through the excess heaven dust
And set it back upon the tongue again

The bread was another matter altogether
Though it lived in there as well

Prayer

        Even
to write about prayer
        is to stand
        knock-kneed and shivering
        with
palms of real flesh crossed
        like
living fig leaves over
    one's real
Privates

            — the baldness of a Naked Nun
            ready for the
            Raping and the suggestions of
            The Lewd Friar
            as he hustles
            out of his robe —

O deadly to set such talk as this
stalking into public view

The breath of the living thing
if indeed it lives will catch and falter

        To nose
into the underbrush of
everybody's hunger
        and say,
parting the bushes,
        here is a Nude Prayer
breeding
        in a dark hour where it
        may spawn

is as
	unconscionable and as brazen as
	vocal prayer in
Unison—
		Everybody doing it
		all together

But who doesn't know
the proper place and
		who hasn't heard of the closet
		and what goes on there—the rich
cloistered piety

Who exhorts? who savours?
who cajoles? who wheedles?
who, faithless
		urges the titillating
		fanfaronade otherwise?

Who needs to mouth and taste so much
what the air is flying full of
at all times
anyway?

An Elusive One

This poem

>can be called a masterpiece
>of the engraver's art

a toupee

>to cover the baldness of man's soul
>drawn with six sure lines

this poem

>sighs like the gaped mouth
>on a monumental granite bas-relief

sings

>like the ding ding ding at
>the checkout counter on a busy Saturday

wallows

>in its own made and set-down completeness
>like a concrete pig in a real sty

runs

>so far ahead of the praise the world
>would give it it is gone

We dug up an old jug, cleaned it, and put it to use

I kiss the mouth
Of this stone jug
Not knowing
Whose lips kissed it last

Or when it was
Though maybe fifty
Years or more

I would not wish
To kiss direct
The mouth of any man
Let alone one putrid in the grave

Instead I find myself
Saluting thus
Through intervening mouths
The man who loved the jug

And love as men love
Through all time and loss
By kissing only that
Which other lips have loved

Landscape as Tune

This stone happening to lodge at the edge of this one
unpaved woodroad dead-ending at the foot of a ragged mountain
is called piety

Similar in appearance to its thousands of grey neighbors
it was kicked here by a horse's hoof in 1873 and has remained since
then to all intents and purposes inert

Strange to say it is hard by what your grandfather if he
was of a poetical turn might have called a laughing brook and hard
by the laughing brook it still exists

It does not exist as a granite teardrop of the gods as an
unloved domestic pearl of great price or as the lumpy dropping
of a stonebird no one can change that

On the other hand it has escaped the scrutiny of the learned
professor the scorn of the worldly and in no way has been
singled out or shat on by fierce animals it freezes and thaws
with the seasons

It has neither grown nor diminished much in all of its
plausible history nor has it a mind to to tell the truth simply
it is grey it is lonesome it is mindless it is unlovely smoke
comes and goes on the mountain

The chance is minute but it is yet a chance that it could
be picked up and carried in a small boy's pocket all the way to
the sea but even if that were to happen it would be of little
consequence

Mind you I did not say that the stone is piety I said it
was called piety and so far as I know I am the only creature to
have called it such in the history of the world and even I
have done that only once

Besides I have called the stone that only in my frivolity
and could as easily have called it smudge or another stone
turniphead or the shining mudpuddle with the butterflies over
it Yokahama

Furthermore now that I think of it I am not very confident
that I ever did call it that but only dreamt that I did so that
what I record here may be but an ill-remembered dream

Municipal Water

Sachems and Potentates
Governors Admirals
Vaziers Bishops and Ambassadors

All of you resplendent
In the colors of your mighty trades

> You, bejeweled ancient Pope
> Riding a white charger
> And exhaling the incensed
> Breath of your power

> You, dancing minister
> To a queen who loved boldness
> And wished you to dance
> Glittering

Your voices tonight, all of them,
In the muffled babble
Of worldly parlay
Making the noises they once made
To settle destinies

Lie at the bottom of my frozen well
Out there in the yard

The wellhouse under the piled drifts
The drifts smooth and unbroken

Such waters as nourish me now
Have long ago been piped in from elsewhere

*   *   *

It is a world of shaggy crystal and black velvet winter
Not a soul abroad at this hour
The traffic on the highway having taken all the people home
Who cared to go

The clanking orange plow and the nightriding plowman
Harrow other precincts where concourse is greater

All surfaces congeal and glisten hard
As a moon begins to appear

I stand by my sink in the night
With a tumbler in hand
Ready to draw what there is from the tap
Ready and sweet
Wholesome municipal water

And hear perhaps because the hour is late
The seismic voices throbbing up
From those deep and unused veins
In the warmer earth below
Which thread like hairy roots everywhere under us

The broken words, merged and echoing
Repeat:

Glory, Death, Glory,
Glory, Victory, Death,
Glory, Glory, Glory

Naming the Names So We Know What They Are

These 15
Hens in the
Yard are
15 demons
Each with
2 undying eyes
30 undying eyes
In all and all
15 have the
Runoftheplace

I know all their
Names which I
Set down here
To brood upon
Like 15 eggs
& they know I
Know their 15
Names

Which are in order
#1 Swillhole the Black
#2 Pain with Points and Edges
#3 Gagalot
#4 Slacksinew
#5 Jeering Bloodshot

(That many being sisters in one family,
perhaps the worst) and

#6 The little orphan Squirmspasm

and now for the rest:

#7 Feeble Windsigh
#8 Pukedandy
#9 Grey Tremor
#10 Bonerot
#11 Slivershove
#12 Feverball
#13 Wartcluster the Populous
#14 Smear
#15 Spinesnap the Limp

And believe me
Their eggs are
Everywhere and
The cock on the dungheap
Who else but the false Jesus
Christ whose other
Name is Awful Sunrise
Or Brainleak the
Plausible

Contemplative Cake

We talked under the streetlamps
About the word, "yearning,"

And about the universe in which
There was need to say such a thing.

Before we were through
The moon she hauled her way
Through quite an arc,

A tomcat on the next street over
Began to yowl.

You could, I suppose,
Call it a wasted evening,
Saying, "see you around,"
And catching the last bus home,

But the cake I ate that night
In the kitchen

Was damned contemplative cake—

Damned contemplative cake.

Uncle Sim on the Last Run to the Great City

I believe he said it,
And there are those
Who say they know for sure
He did since they
Knew someone who was there
As passenger on the
Last run he took.
But there's not anyone
Who couldn't see him anyhow,
Moving with perfect footing
Through the swaying aisles in his
Immaculate blue-black uniform
Punching tickets like he owned
The company himself
And only let those ride who
Met his satisfaction as
Deserving of the honor —
Or hear him clear his throat
For the last time as she
Comes squeaking and hissing
Into the great yards and call
From car to car,
"All out for whoredom
Claps and crabs
And the swamps of vice and sin!
All out for Sodom and
Gomorrah and scarlet
Flaming
Babylon!"

from *Twelvebelly the Ogre*

I have thought all day of the giant butterfly
Twelvebelly keeps behind roof-high glass in his great hall.
Argent and crimson it is with a wingspan of five feet or more
And a head the size of an orange.

Did it live once, this double kite-sized creature
With silvered wings that throw back the gleams of candle and flare
In the hands of scuttling servants?

Or is it rather a cunningly crafted gift from some
Artisan of the countryside, who strove with febrile mind
To conceive and then execute a gift worthy of an ogre?

It would be better if Twelvebelly would say to us
Talking loosely in his cups some night
Some such words as these: "I remember well the year
Of the great butterfly hunt," or

"Speaking as we were of craftsmen, you may take as example
My great butterfly in the hall."

But rather he enjoys, I think, in silence
The quizzical glances and gape-mouthed stares
Of all who must tread his long hallway wondering.

I have been wondering myself which I should prefer,
The prodigious larva and gigantic pupation
Happening in the real green woods of the world

Or the clank of grotesque hatching at the forge
And the hope that here is something at last
Monstrous enough to appease.

Twelvebelly's After Dinner Music

After he has barbecued
And picked clean the bones
Of what I'd rather not describe
But leave to your imagination
Twelvebelly belches like
A distant battlefield of cannons
And retires to his comfortable den.

There he reaches under the lid
Of his hinged-top elephant's foot
Hassock and withdraws his
Gleaming concertina
Adorned with silky tassels
And inlaid ivory flanks.

Oh wonder be upon us
He will,
As frequently he does,
Raise his voice in hearty song
Of melancholy woe
And vibrant booming beauty
All compounded.

The breathless listening hearts
Are all but one spasmodic throb,
As the music,
Expansion and contraction
From the pumping of those mighty arms
Is mingled with his sobbing bass.

The words?
They would not bear repeating here,
But the hour grows later
And later still
As on and on he plays and sings,
And the tears of his eyes,
They are as of Deucalion's flood,
And flow as deep and long.

From *Twelvebelly the Ogre*

The cook in Twelvebelly's kitchen
Master of the great vats
Like Scheherazade lives on
By his wits
Cramming the maw of the future
With novelty after novelty
But unlike her
Has in reserve one final trick
When his purview is exhausted at last
And the domains are plundered
Of all that might serve as viands

He may with one leap of grandeur
Surpass each prior invention
And offer himself as ingredient

Ah what taste so jaded as not to relish
A fricassee that has in part
Invented itself

Woods

I Mapshape

I do not believe this woods is star-shaped
Potato fields and settlements pushing
  Into its five fringed crotches

Nor is it colonnaded anywhere
In and throughout its formless extent
  With alleys to duck in and out of

Nor a wobbly melted trapezoid
Marked only with buried stakes and dead trees
  Daubed blazes on vanished surfaces

No not even that much shapeless shape
A cloud that you say looks like a turkey
  Or a cow's ear bent by the wind

Isn't it more similar to the sight
Of the inside of a crumpled paper bag
  When you peep in with a flashlight

A stop-action photo of underwear
For a family of five at the window
  Of the big laundromat dryer

Yes I think you would have to agree
And immeasurably more is being there
  Without map or aerial view

Being inside is like shouting o hell
At a bingo game where you never win
  Never have more than four in a row

II   Some History

Fragonard never saw the New Brunswick woods
So far as I know,
But I sometimes wish he had,
And not for reasons you might think

Consider how he could have ridden in
Behind the oxen
Perched on some rig made just for the occasion,
Swinging his lunch pail of ultramarine and gold filagree,
With his quiver of brushes slung over his shoulder
Like the maiden Artemis
Off to the hunt.

Do you think that I would want to bring him in
Just to see him shit his silken pantaloons
At the sudden sight of a giant cowmoose
Slurping up lilypads
Like an ill-mannered boarder?
No sir.

I'd like to see what would have happened
When he began to twitch his brush
With the delicate touch of the woodsman
Twitching logs,
See him move his space and light
According to sudden gougings of new sky
When the first great trees went thundering down,
See his elbows and shoulders begin
To work with fury
Rather than his fingertips and wrists.

And, besides, what he could have left to us
Would be good to have as well,
Some of the delicacies—even ours—
That history keeps on throwing away:
The elegant slouch of tired men in wet wool
Grouped in a tableau they fell into once
In early firelight outdoors,
A twenty-second picnic in the luminous slush,
Someone writing a letter in the camps
With a stub-fingered curlicue flourish
Of a signature that looked pretty good,

The poised weight of a gleaming axehead
Babied to a razor edge
Descending, to prove the point of craft,
Upon a mere as yet unshaven hair.

III   Owners

Those can't be dreamwoods you're talking about,
Those are my woods, ugly and matted and scraggy
Though they be. I've been lost in them before.

You've been lost in my dreamwoods then,
Where so many places look just alike
And tow roads go around in circles.
You keep on going by the same burnt out camps
Over and over again. Where I come from
You head for low ground and water;
The stream will move to take you out at last,
Or so I used to be told.

The low ground can be swamp, though,
With a slow plug at the bottom,
Hills all around except where you came in,
You feel like a fly in a toilet bowl,
The only way is down the pipe.

Those are my dreamwoods, then,
Even with that business about the fly.
You learn it's nasty having water get still
And then seep underground
And travel where you can't.

You dream nasty then.

Yes, I dream nasty;
You seem to want my dreamwoods
To be full of unicorns and elves.
I tell you I've drifted a chain of empty lakes
And come back and past the spot
Where I think I started over and over, many times.

In your sleep?

Yes, and woke up tired with the
Swamp smell in my nose.

Those are my woods — real woods.

They're my dreamwoods;
I can't help it.

Personal Poem

Some domestic animals
And most of the people I know
(God bless them)

From time to time
May be caught in the act
Of snuffing the air

Hoping to catch
In their flared nostrils
An imponderable musk

Seasonal

The wild turkeys of the night gather on my ceiling
In herds
And meaning no harm, jostle and nudge and pass and repass
Merely feeding.
So bland in my presence they must be feral, they ignore
My raised arm
And keep on being there
By the hundreds.
Though I shut my eyes I can hear them still
Croon and gobble
Croon and gobble
Croon and gobble
Gobble and croon:
A babble of inoffensiveness that ought to induce sleep.
In the morning, after the astringency of unsugared grapefruit
I shall
Gaze at the milk-red banner of the Telegraph-Journal
And squint beyond
To the sun-lit honeycombed snowbanks outside the house,
Happening to wonder,
I suppose,
About this odd touchdown, from God knows what flyway

The Tongue Is a Brush to Colour the Truth

To paint the brown earth mocha
Here where we live
Seems odd — or possibly wrong.

Running the tongue down a long furrow
In a farmer's field
Yields, but yields the flavor
Of potato stones and drenched moss.

Try another crumbling alleyway in the turned earth;
It is still the same
And yet another:
Abrasive porridge
Grained and flecked
Like spewed granite, thought to be wholesome.

Yet the hills
Sloped with age
Are mauve
In the longer light of early Spring;
That is just what they are

Dry and powdery against the lips
Like the outer skin
Of a failed blueberry.

Perhaps the answer lies in this:

The taste of Winter's woods-snow
Melted in a cup
And drunk in Spring
Is bright with invisible history,
Storied particles that merge to
A luminous wash
For the belly of the eye.

The Names I Would Dare Give Myself:

He who has spots on his shirt
And fails to recall what
He has imperfectly eaten

Who knew brightness and lustre of days
Maybe — prove that he didn't

Ran errands to the store
Brought back the right change
And forgot no items

And a walker of the streets of the town
From time to time at noon
Because he had somewhere to go

He with eyes focussed
On the magical meaningful buns
In the bakery window — why not?

And a looker-around in crowds
For familiar faces only —
Again — why not?

From the Middle of the River

If it only could be permitted
I would aspire to some such title
As a Chinese painter once gave to himself,
Among many others:
"The informal historian of the meandering river."

For I might wish to say to you
As a strong man does in his youth,
"In my time I see them
From my station midway over the bridge
Some of the lesser fish, perhaps, mere shadows
Desiring the sea."

—will sometimes turn and for an instant
Expose a flank to the sun in the ceaseless dark pouring.
Such rare flashing and going I would see and say.
But the only title I dare take now in my aging
Is he,
The old man who goes on forever lying.

Roadhockey

The roadhockey game out under our window
Is like the Chinese soup
With grandfather cabbages thrown in
Decades before
It simmers through the years
As the bulbs in the streetlamps
Have been replaced a hundred times since it began

Enter the fray my little son
Little onion into the stew
The original ingredients have long since been devoured
But they have left their legacy:
The game itself, a roiling flowing two-sided thing
And a meaningless astronomical score

In the Park

I'll tell you where we are:
We've somehow got ourselves
Inside that monument at the park,
You know the one I mean,
The gigantic horse with some general
Riding on it

No wonder there's no lights in here
No one's supposed to be in it at all
For any purposes whatever
It doesn't even need to be cleaned out
Or tended to in any way I'm afraid
We're in here for good

Right now I think we're standing
In the hind right hoof so if
We hoist ourselves up onto this ledge
And crawl forward on our bellies
We might at least look out at the world
Through the eyes of this old warhorse
Which I suppose we might as well do
To pass the time

Report from Paradise

The first thing that hits you
Is how much like the movies it is,
Wading around in some cloudy stuff
Up to your knees wondering about it all
Until you-know-who in a white suit
Comes along and gives you the answers
And makes you feel at home.

"This is it, Harry," he says, "Paradise,
And you just call the shots the way you want."

So it's off to the dogtracks in Florida for a while
With plenty of women and all that sort of thing,
One side trip out into the Gulf
To have a look at a hurricane at sea
And a real honest-to-God waterspout
Then on the way back a glimpse into
A shrimp-packing plant which is
More interesting than you might suppose.

Now the way time is
Or isn't I should say I guess,
I haven't yet made duty calls
To all the relatives the way I ought,
But when I do I will have
Just arrived and get the credit for being
A loving heart and loyal boy.

The thing I like about eternity
Is the marvelous way it's set up and arranged;
It covers everything and yet
Any damn fool there ever was
Can understand the way it works.

Oh, there is one fact I've noticed
That might seem strange to you,
I'm not left-handed anymore,
But equally good,
Perfect you might say,
With either hand or foot.

For this Day

Avoid strangers
Avoid friends
Avoid relatives

Beware of animals

Enjoy the
Chugging neutral
Throb
Of bland functionaries

Enjoy filling out
A form

Enjoy doing only
An average
Job of it

A Nocturnal Misunderstanding

Wait, I am only
The windowdresser
Dressing the window
I am not for sale
And the window is not
Ready for you to
Look through at what
Is in here yet
I am bald and aging
And am supposed to disappear
Before you begin
To desire the tasteful
Things I lay out for you
If I thought you
Would be so full of
Money and lust as to take
The first thing you
See I would at
Least have worn
A clean shirt and
A modish hairpiece
And been worth the
Price or at any rate
I could have made
It look that way

II. Short Stories

Uncollected

Pig-of-the-Wind: A Fragment from the Archives

Ollie can tell you much about Pig-of-the-Wind because it was to him that Pig-of-the-Wind appeared. To him only. And because only to him, it is to him we go for what we know of Pig-of-the-Wind. And too, the red-eyed stinger, but mostly Pig-of-the-Wind. It happened to Ollie first when he was a small boy and subsequently only a few more times.

Ollie would run home to his house each time, but once in a while there was a strong, almost brutal wind blowing off the brown and green hills and right on to his back. It would seem almost to be pushing him home, off the road and in through the front door of his house. Only once every two or three years, and then only, did this powerful wind have anything to do with Pig-of-the-Wind. Before learning about Pig-of-the-Wind, we must learn about the powerful winds and what they were like and what Ollie thought about them. Pig-of-the-Wind is concerned with Ollie a few of those times where there were strong winds blowing at his back from down the brown and green hills. Pig-of-the-Wind has nothing to do with anything else in the whole world — that is, for all we know.

We must know first of all that Ollie was never troubled by winds over most of his route. Only the last part of his journey home when he came out of the forest road and into the open space. Here it was, though the wind could thrash the tops of the trees in the forest itself, did the wind really show its strength — coming down over the hills and always from behind Ollie, pushing him upwards and homewards so that he had no choice but to go faster and faster. Arriving home on these occasions, Ollie found he was without the power of speech, but that mattered very little to him and surely matters, for that reason, even less to us, who are mostly interested in Pig-of-the-Wind, or at the very most about Pig-of-the-Wind and the red-eyed-stinger.

In the open space where there were still a few trees, the wind these few times would bend the tops of those few trees all the way to the ground. Ollie could see that and see also that the wind was not just air moving, but stuff—like sea-blue molasses—pushing in fingers and curls of living substance. Another thing that always happened: Ollie, you must know, was never without his wide red straw hat; on those occasions we are speaking of, the wind never blew Ollie's hat from his head. Ollie thought about this whenever he thought later, as he often did, about the wind. He decided this: the wind pushed him so rapidly toward his house that it could not have pushed his red hat any faster than he himself was going. The wind was so strong that it mattered very little how big or how little anything was that happened to be in its path. Also, when he thought about it, Ollie would think how lucky he was that the wind pushed him home instead of in some other direction—for instance, out into the bay where there were sharks or to the hut of the brutal agricultural agent.

Perhaps the fourth or maybe the fifth time the wind pushed Ollie home as fast as it could have blown his red straw hat, Ollie looked back at the thick wind and saw the face of Pig-of-the-Wind. Pig-of-the-Wind was pushing the wind that was pushing Ollie; behind the Pig-of-the-Wind perhaps pushing him or helping him to push the wind was the red-eyed-stinger. But Ollie was never clear about the red-eyed-stinger; about Pig-of-the-Wind there could be no mistake. You must remember that these winds were made of a stuff—not like ordinary wind. Now Pig-of-the-Wind was more clearly and solidly made of stuff, somewhat pinkish, than the bluish wind. Pig-of-the-Wind was not part of the wind; he was more solid than the wind, and he was pushing it.

There is very little else to tell about what happened. After the first time Ollie always looked over his shoulder to see Pig-of-the-Wind. Each time one of those great winds blew, Pig-of-the-Wind was there. Perhaps five or six times in all. Ollie had one frightening dream about Pig-of-the-Wind, but he never thought that was very important. He never forgot it though. Here we will discuss the dream separately and concentrate upon Ollie's thoughts about those few times that Pig-of-the-Wind actually appeared to him.

Right here it ought to be said that in a relatively long life Ollie thought a great deal about Pig-of-the-Wind, and about very little else that is worth recording. Thus, Ollie's thoughts about Pig-of-the-Wind are somewhat systematized and much digested here. Ollie was not a literate man; so it is perhaps losing something of the authentic nature of his thought process to condense to reporting what originally was a full and slow ripening of speculation. Since Ollie is, so far as we know, the only creature ever to have seen Pig-of-the-Wind, and really the only person ever to have spent any time thinking about Pig-of-the-Wind, his experience and subsequent thought on the matter constitute the full body of human knowledge about Pig-of-the-Wind. Seldom is an investigator of any subject so fortunate as to have so clearly circumscribed a subject.

One of the things that Ollie thought about very often was the question of whether Pig-of-the-Wind ever pushed the wind down over the hills at a time when he, Ollie, was somewhere else. At night Ollie would lie in bed and listen for the great rush of that thick blue stuff, so that he might know that Pig-of-the-Wind was abroad. But though there were storms, and some strong ones too, Ollie never heard a wind that he could honestly say was really like those when he was on the road and Pig-of-the-Wind appeared. Once or twice he even got out of bed and went to the door just to make sure; on those occasions when he actually had a chance to find out, he was disappointed to find only an ordinary wind. He became satisfied soon that he would never learn whether or not Pig-of-the-Wind were abroad when he was not. He never gave up wondering, though. Dependent as we are on Ollie for knowledge of Pig-of-the-Wind, and since Ollie has now been dead some dozen years, it is safe to say that we can never learn for sure either.

A question closely related to this one is whether or not Pig-of-the-Wind ever pushed winds anywhere else but where Ollie saw him. Ollie felt that Pig-of-the-Wind clearly was not living at the top of the brown and green hills, because he always saw him very high up in the sky. He somehow did not seem to be part of the earthly world of Ollie's village and its surroundings, so that his appearance in other places seemed plausible enough. Ollie's problem here was to try to imagine other places. Somehow when Ollie tried to think about Pig-of-the-Wind apart from himself on the road on the way home, he was unable to. Yet he spent many an hour trying to do just that. For some reason it seemed to Ollie that he ought to try to imagine Pig-of-the-Wind pushing some other person home in some other place. All his life Ollie never gave up trying this, and feeling this obligation, but he was never able to do what he thought, for some reason, he ought to do.

There was to Ollie the discomforting matter of the name. Though he only once in his life allowed his lips to form the syllables "Pig-of-the-Wind" and this once to his everlasting sorrow in the presence of the brutal agricultural agent, he knew, he hoped, in his mind, that "Pig-of-the-Wind" was the proper name. He thought about the possibilities of alternatives, though, wondering even as he thought whether thinking in this fashion might not be improper. Improper or not, there was little he could do as the suggestions of alternatives came into his head — especially at night as he waited for sleep to come to him.

The most compelling of these thoughts was this: The name "Pig-of-the-Wind" seemed to say that the wind was more important than the Pig, when from Ollie's position of looking over his shoulder, it appeared that the wind was coming from in front of the Pig, impelled forward by it, so to speak. In that case shouldn't the name be "Wind-of-the-Pig"? Ollie, as we have noted before, was an unsophisticated man and would not have been able to consider the subtleties of different uses of the genitive case, differences that, could he have known them, might have relieved his anxiety to some extent. As it was, to Ollie the distinction between the name "Pig-of-the-Wind" and the name "Wind-of-the-Pig" was like the differences between, on the one hand, a well-fitting pair of trousers, confining but not binding and above all decent, and, on the other hand, a tattered and decaying pair, threatening always to catch and sunder upon the merest thorn bush and expose him to shame. Other names he thought of were "Pig-Wind" and "Wind-Pig." These names were as perilous to his mind as "Wind-of-the-Pig." For some reason the name of the red-eyed-stinger never gave his mind a moment's uneasiness.

Before telling about the one time that Ollie said the name "Pig-of-the-Wind" aloud, we ought to relate another incident concerning names. Once when Ollie was still fairly young, he had far too much to drink at a party that he and his friends arranged in one of the village warehouses after hours. Ollie had been sitting up against a stack of crates for a long while, feeling more and more the effects of what he had drunk. Soon into his head popped several new names, names that made him laugh uproariously. The first of these was "bacon-blower." Then a veritable torrent of names rushed into his mind as he blushed, tittered, laughed, and even wept at the ease with which new names came into his head: "Hamfat-hurricane," "Pork-puffer," and dozens more. Ollie's friends tried to get him to tell what he was laughing at, since many seemed to think he was laughing at them; though nothing could have been farther from the truth, Ollie refused to say what was funny.

There was nothing funny, however, about the time Ollie spoke aloud the name, "Pig-of-the-Wind." It is now time to tell what can be known about that particular incident. It happened a few days after Ollie's hysterical and drunken experiments in thinking of other names as he sat with his friends in the darkened warehouse. For a few days after the party Ollie went about his daily rounds with chastened spirit and downcast manner. With his unfailing sense of whom to persecute and when to victimize, the brutal agricultural agent appeared to read a discomfort and a weakness into Ollie's more than usually quiet behavior. He showered upon Ollie an unending stream of veiled abuse and subtle allusions to the irregularities of Ollie's domestic arrangements. With no more reason than that he found at last another indignity more than he could bear, Ollie spoke to his persecutor in cracked and angry voice the words he was to brood about so much in later years. The agent had said no more to him than, "… chickens like you probably have in your little yard," when Ollie cursed him aloud, invoking as he did so, Pig-of-the-Wind. As near as Ollie could remember his reply had been, "Pig-of-the-Wind will blow you into the bay and you will be eaten by the sharks." It was that very night that the agent was killed in the great warehouse fire. On the edge of the crowd that had gathered in the middle of the night to watch the great red and orange blaze, Ollie shook in fear at what he had possibly done. The next morning his stomach cramped uncontrollably as he watched the charred body of the agent raked out of the still-smoking ashes and borne in a litter past the onlookers—some weeping, some silent, all wondering what the demise of the agent would mean to them.

In the years after the fire Ollie had even more to think about, more than just wondering what it was exactly that he had said to the agent. He began to entertain the thought that he might on some future occasion, when his temper was sufficiently roused, give way and invoke Pig-of-the-Wind once more, perhaps again with some dreadful result—or perhaps with no perceivable result at all. Ollie wondered about this so much that on a couple occasions at least he came close to trying out the power of invocation, not in anger but merely to satisfy his curiosity. He proposed to himself the plan of choosing a deserted place on the road to the village; then when he encountered a bird or insect or even a snake, he would curse it in order to observe the results. Ollie never carried this plan into effect, however, for he remembered that the brutal agricultural agent had not, indeed, been blown out into the bay and eaten by sharks but instead had perished in the flames of the great warehouse fire. As fortune would have it, Ollie neither experimented coolly with the invocation to Pig-of-the-Wind nor was for the rest of his life ever taunted by anyone sufficiently to arouse his anger.

Ollie's declining years were, for all anyone could observe, tranquil beyond most men's dreams. So it seemed, at least, to many who passed by his house in the evening, seeing him out in his yard about his chores, occasionally casting an eye to the far horizon and then to the very heights of the deepening sky.

Finally there is the matter of the dream — a subordinate matter, perhaps; but then, in an affair so perplexing as the present one, nothing should be omitted, especially since Ollie has passed on and cannot testify beyond what has in good fortune come to these pages. Nothing outstanding about the time of the dream or about Ollie's activities on the days immediately preceding the dream can be discovered. The dream itself was brief, vivid, memorable. Ollie felt himself blown by the wind as usual on the road to his home. Looking over his shoulder, he was chilled to discover that though the viscous, blue air was pushing him, there was no sign of Pig-of-the-Wind, or of the red-eyed-stinger for that matter. More horrifying still, the wind pushed Ollie not to his house as it usually did but high into the air. For most of the journey up into the air Ollie's heels felt higher than his head, but after a while his sense of up and down became thoroughly muddled. He was finally aware of moving into a kind of funnel, the walls of which were composed of thousands of long webby filaments. At last in the depths of the funnel, at the very center, smaller at first but growing larger by the second, was the distorted countenance of Pig-of-the-Wind. Ollie perceived this and understood almost immediately after — the face of Pig-of-the-Wind was distorted because the cheeks were not puffed out as they had been whenever Ollie had seen them before; now they were huge concave dimples — Pig-of-the-Wind was sucking him in rather than, as had always been the case before, blowing him about. Just before Ollie awoke, he was stunned by a great voice booming all about him as he sped toward the gigantic pig face, "I WILL SWALLOW THE ENTIRE UNIVERSE!" The dream included no glimpse of the red-eyed-stinger.

*   *   *

I realize that what I have put down here upon paper is a far cry from what one would usually expect to find in an annual agricultural report. If the commission wishes a full report in the usual sense of the word, it may simply refer to the reports of previous years and alter the date to the current one. The principal conclusions may be the same as they have been for every one of the twenty-one years I have been here: that is, the community will never adapt sufficiently to make the growing of soybeans a profitable venture. The commission may never—ever—look forward to a time when this God-forsaken little corner of the world will be economically self-sufficient. Furthermore, and I hereby state that this annual report is my last word on the whole matter, the mystery of the great warehouse fire which caused the demise of my predecessor will never be solved—ever. I assert here for the last time what I have asserted in every previous report: that my predecessor was brutal beyond credibility and Ollie, as I have seen fit to name him in my reports, is so far from having been guilty as to have been instead, saintly in the face of persecution from both his fellow villagers and from me, the appointed avenger, as it were, of my wretched precursor. Ollie, for all we know, may have been one of the few in our days to whom the gift of prophecy, or perhaps prophetic vision I should say, was given. Such considerations I see at last far outweigh in importance any such trifling concerns as soybeans, fertilizers, warehouses, or even the puny matter of bringing to justice a local arsonist, who himself in last analysis may well have been performing a higher act of justice than we ourselves have been endeavoring to effect.

I have said that Ollie's later years were tranquil beyond most men's dreams. And so they were, even in the face of persecution. It was this very attribute which first caught my attention when I was forced in my official capacity to badger Ollie with one interrogation after another. Little by little I became more concerned with the radiant spiritual quality of my suspect than with any performance of my duties—and justly so I will maintain. I freely admit now that for over sixteen years I have been wholly derelict in what the manual defines as my duties; but I have been faithful, indeed, perhaps at great cost to my own welfare, in chronicling higher matters—for in such directions did my interrogations inevitably and irresistably tend. And, if you wonder why I write so frankly—I dare say you will deem also so irrationally—let me say that I have contracted what the villagers here describe as the dreaded autumn fevers, and my end is, unless some miracle intervene, very near. Who would write of soybeans and fertilizers at such a time? Who would, alone in a far corner of the earth among people who are strangers to him really, not wish to make some accounting at last? I certainly look forward to a death less violent than that of my miserable predecessor. His abuse of Ollie seems to me now, so much did I worship that good man at last, a horrible sacrilege. May I also, but only in the interests of a higher justice and through no personal malice whatever: May Pig-of-the-Wind blow the commission off the face of the earth.

You may by this time no longer be reading what I write and instead are scurrying about to find an emergency replacement for me. That is of little concern to me now. As I recall regulations, however, it will be required that my full report be posted and be a matter of record for all time. So too will this document be read when my estate comes to be settled; I have seen to that. Well then, hail to you, minor clerk, statistician, secretary, or archives superintendent of the future! If Pig-of-the-Wind has not blown you all to oblivion or has spared the universe and has not as yet sucked it all up into his holy porcine gut, stay with me for a bit; take this volume of the Agricultural Reports with you on your lunch hour, and we will speculate together on the most sublime truths. For you I have first of all a special confession. Before that, however, let me say that the more you read about Pig-of-the-Wind, Ollie, and yes, me, because I am deeply implicated, the more, though infinitessimally more, it becomes true that Pig-of-the-Wind begins his long, protracted but sure swallowing of the universe. I am joshing a bit here, though somewhat wryly, for I myself, now so little an agricultural agent and so almost completely bound up in thoughts of Pig-of-the-Wind, am myself almost wholly swallowed. But to the confession. It is this: at no time did Ollie tell me in so many words anything concerning his experience with Pig-of-the-Wind or with the red-eyed-stinger.

**This report is continued in Volumes XXV and
XXVI of the Agricultural Reports.**

Never Bet on a Dead Horse

Under the shadow of the cliff, where the rays of the moon could not reach, it was as dark as the inside of a coat closet. Frank and Orville were happy enough about that, I can tell you, for their business there was not such as they wished anyone to see.

"Hold your end of it up, you bastard," cried Frank irritably.

"I am holding it up—I am," came the muffled reply.

High atop the cliff stood a close-packed grove of tall oaks. Their leaves, dry and dead but clinging still to the branches, were silvery in the eerie light and spoke as with a thousand tongues, rattling in the gusts of night wind. Out on the water, beyond where the two men had anchored their small craft, the crisped surface shone with an answering luminosity.

"Chink chink." The sound came from the impenetrable darkness between the two vast areas of lighted night landscape—as if shovels were being hurriedly used in loose gravelly soil along the shore.

"I don't mind telling you I'm scared," said one voice.

"Shut up," came the reply, "and keep your mind on that valve."

On the further shore, across the bay, the blue donkey lights in the familiar "V" pattern winked on and off.

"You notice Robinson ain't here."

"Robinson's not the only one not here."

"But you notice who is here, don't you?"

There are not enough shades of silver or hues and tints of black for any painter to convey the sublety of this night scene, but it did exist once upon a time, be assured of that.

Unnumbered, likewise, are the qualms, fears, and petty hopes in the hearts of Frank and Orville as they lunged, heaved, manipulated, and followed the patterned movements of their task.

Unbeknownst to Orville and Frank, anchored a few yards up toward the head of the bay, but well under the protective shadow of the cliff, was a sleek expensive motor launch, the small waves lapping against its side. Inside, under this soiled rain coat crouched Leland Watrous, viewing the scene from the same prospective as I give it to you. Indeed, it is possible that I am Leland Watrous, but if this is true, how do I know of the fear that grips the hearts of Frank and Orville, unless possibly I am Faye Watrous, Leland's wife, overseeing one of his dreams, after having listened to so many?

Not a cloud shifts; the wind neither dies nor freshens. The lighting remains the same dramatic chiaroscuro, when suddenly it is clear what Orville and Frank are doing. How the truth often comes like that, unbidden as can be! Those rogues are digging up the body of a dead trotting horse named Parishioner and are resuscitating him so that he may be entered in the races at the fairgrounds tomorrow.

"O God, what a night," Leland says. "I spent it cramped up under my raincoat in a motor launch."

"It was an act of cowardice, pure and simple," Faye replies, bringing him coffee. "Robinson should have been there."

II

In the shipping room where he works, Leland feels the results of his arduous night. His aching muscles he complains of to his co-workers in this wise — as if explanations were necessary: "At my age it takes all night to do what I used to do all night." As he says this he digs his elbow into the ribs of Walter Carson, who is uninterested in Leland's leering allusions, but is close by in order to double check the waterflow settings on his labelling machine.

Later, he pondered what the word "raincoat" had to do with either Leland's unimaginable sex life or the task at hand. Faye would understand, no doubt, but Walter was not acquainted with her.

Above, along the rim of the grandstand roof snapped and fluttered thousands of gaily-coloured pennants; except in the cavernous shadow created by this amply-proportioned structure, the sun touched all the world with the brilliant illumination of its metallic golden rays. The infield shimmered and lost much of its inherent green under the solar brilliance. The track itself, despite the salubrious effects of a light morning shower, seemed bleached to chalky dust. It was kicked into powdery little clouds by the wind.

"You can't stay away can you Lee?" came a friendly call from several rows back up in the gloom.

And then another voice, "Hey Lee. Another loser?"

The laughter from up there was friendly and joshing, and Watrous responded to it with a waggling of his hand in the air, but with no twisting around or peering back into what could not be seen.

The hum of the crowd was a monotonous, slow, happy crescendo, and the day passed further beyond its meridian. Soon it would happen, though few but Watrous knew. The tout sheets had no clue of it, what with their comfortable orthodoxies, nor did the great board know either, the name "Parishioner" appearing ordinarily—nor did the barking voice of the public address, intoning "Parishioner" with no more quality to it than it accorded "Waterspout," "Dan's Lady," or "Opera Buff."

"Oh, man, a dead horse! There's something frightening in that, you know." Had the bones retained sufficient strength or the sinews any renewable flexion to perform for so long as this race would require? How he would love to have told Faye the whole story—even Walter Carson, for that matter, poor Walter whose thumb had been caught under a ream of heavy brown stock because he could not mind his own business. What knowledge a man might learn from crouching in a motor launch all night under a raincoat, while the blue donkey lights flashed on the far shore! Watrous knew he had mortgaged his sanity to bet on this one.

"They're off!" And the mobile starting gate folded its great wings and sped forward and off the track ahead of the mincing nags, the sure winner in any such race.

On the sulky, Robinson looked far more cadaverous than Parishioner. "Damned clever job," thought Watrous. "I'll bet that Robinson is terrified; he sure looks it."

Does the sun conspire with its brilliance to mask the truth? Does it flash upon the whirring spokes with such intensity as to divert all eyes and allay suspicion? Watrous could read the expression on Robinson's tiny face, nonetheless, even from such a distance — grinning like a skeleton up above the fiery flash of his chariot: it was terror and terror alone.

Somewhere in the crowd were Frank and Orville, and here, where his friends could see him was Leland Watrous, who knew, though Frank and Orville didn't know he knew, what they knew

Exhilaration, pure and unalloyed.

My God, the dead nag, Parishioner, look at him go! Three lengths ahead and no one the wiser.

In her kitchen Faye Watrous prepares a supper of meatloaf and baked potatoes, thinking to herself, "I'll be damned glad when this day is over."

In the shipping room Walter Carson stares at his bandaged thumb and muses, "I may have a bandaged thumb, but by Jesus, I wouldn't be in his shoes for anything."

III

The shops are closing; the traffic begins to move out of town into the country. Good God, what time has it gotten to be? Walter Carson, though it isn't his job, drapes the machines with their protective coverings and then checks the main power switch. "Good night, my beauties," he says, enjoying his little joke.

Frank and Orville, those rascals, are now miles from the fairgrounds, miles from anywhere near here at all, and only the devil himself knows what shady business they may be up to next. They seemed to learn at some time during the long afternoon — a long, long race, didn't anybody notice? — that something was going wrong. They fled the scene hours ago in the interests of their own safety and freedom.

At the far turn in the late afternoon Parishioner is out all alone leading the field. But all of them, Parishioner, Waterspout, Dan's Lady, Opera Buff, and the rest glide, as if in slow motion, as if they are moving in congealing taffy. Watrous notices and wonders why the crowd, now growling like voices on a record undergoing inexplicable deceleration, reacts as it does. The hills and valleys along the flapping flags move across their cloth fields with stately and more and more ponderous grandeur.

With events transpiring at such a pace the crowd must be able to see what Leland Watrous sees—with a slumping heart: a ribbony thing flapping from the right front leg of Parishioner and the flash of white bone showing through. It gets longer and longer and then falls away. But a worse thing happens yet (Oh how long will Frank and Orville lie low now?) even as another fluttering ribbon begins to detach itself from Parishioner's flank. Robinson sees what is happening and fatally starts up, jerking like a rag doll and flopping back just as quickly, to tumble from his sulky onto the track in a heap, even as a massive gobbet of Parishioner's flesh falls away exposing a good portion of his ribcage; but still Parishioner rides on, his bones baring themselves all to the pitiless sun.

Robinson had died of fright; no man there could doubt it. If he had not, he soon would have been pummeled to death by the onrushing hooves of Waterspout, Dan's Lady, Opera Buff, and the rest. Though he is becoming more and more denuded, Parishioner retains his perfect form; he neither breaks nor falters, even with the unmanned sulky veering and racketting along behind.

Robinson dead, Watrous is aghast at finding his bankroll and his all riding on the white flashing bones of a proud skeleton, who, even should he maintain his lead, will undoubtedly be disqualified (Frank and Orville may thank their lucky stars they are so far away). The crowd quickens and whistles and cheers. Watrous recalls the sporting taunts of his friends in the darkness behind him and finds himself wondering what they must think. After all, he, Watrous, has placed his bets on a dead horse, and despite all, it may, in a manner of speaking, win yet. Have they been so perspicacious as he? No, they earned not the knowledge of an uncomfortable night in an anchored motor launch, nor would Watrous have shared with them his hard-earned tip. Not in a million years.

So it is with Watrous in the splendid isolation of his terror, assuming that no one else in the crowd has staked so much and is now sharing in the utter collapse. How lucky Walter Carson is, just now pulling into his driveway and noting that his son-in-law's Plymouth is parked there ahead of him. He jauntily hops up his front steps unaware that if he should look behind him, he would see strange murky clouds lying low in the west, over in the direction of the fairgrounds. Happy Walter Carson has even forgotten his bandaged thumb.

Faye, on the other hand, is troubled by distant and forboding awareness; the meatloaf is sizzling on to completion, while she parts the curtains of her Western window and perceives the mysterious lumpy darkening. Hadn't she been the one to put her finger on the flaw? Yes, indeed, for her the matter had been grasped in its essence. She saw now that everything would founder on one bitter rock: Robinson's cowardice.

And now for the last things before the last. The growling waves of sound from the crowd seem in Watrous's ears like a great moaning lamentation, "Another loser, Lee?" Out on the track the chalky white bones of Parishioner streaking into the home stretch begin to fleck off in splinters and bits, these flying shards filling the darkening air and streaming back at the following field like missiles. Opera Buff has been injured in the eye by one of these, it is quite evident; it has caused him to break, and the packed field around him mostly do the same. Confusion prevails.

Watrous knows that the only contest left lies in the question of whether Parishioner will hold together long enough to cross the finish line. He is amazed at how caught up he is in this question, for no matter what happens now he has to all intents and purposes lost. The meatloaf in the oven will wait there forever; he must never sit down and eat it there in his own warm, snug kitchen.

But doubt exists for but a short duration. Before the clattering bones of Parishioner can cross the finish line and confound the judges — before that — the lowering clouds produce a brief shivering blast from their bellies, and the Parishioner who was becomes no more than an ashy blizzard of particles, blown hither and thither like dry leaflets in a dust devil. The progress of the careering sulky is arrested as the shafts bite into the surface of the track. Opera Buff and Dan's Lady, no longer trotting, gallop past in a wild panic, Opera Buff tossing her injured head convulsively. The crowd roars, but Watrous can no longer tell whether it is with joy or dismay.

In his living room Walter Carson is holding his injured thumb aloft in order to make a slightly self-aggrandizing point concerning moral and prudential conduct.

"I may have got myself this sore thumb stupidly," he says to his daughter and son-in-law, "but I sure as Hell would have more sense than to bet on a dead horse."

Across town in the gathering gloom of her unlighted apartment Faye Watrous keeps a lonely vigil. Faithful to the last, she has placed the overdone meatloaf in the warming oven. "What is the good of it all," she thinks. "It does no damned good at all to be right."

And Robinson—whose fate Faye's prediction had so correctly forecasted — his broken little body was removed tenderly by track attendants from where it had been thrown in the remarkable race. If Robinson could speak, he would no doubt answer Faye, "It does no damned good to be wrong either."

And what of Frank and Orville? You may be sure they are, as was said before, far far away, and lying low just long enough to figure out some new kind of scrape to get themselves into. You may also be sure that they have come away from the whole thing scot-free. Bastards like that always do.

From *A Family Album*

This Story Ends in a Pinegrove

1. The Motives Behind Travelling to the Shore, Viewing Wreckage and Flying Kites

If we could, we would always take a trip down to the shore the day after a big storm—gales, and even hurricanes once in a while.

It is of some importance to resist the idea that morbidly we just wanted to see everything smashed and still roaring—small battered boats upside-down in backyards where they didn't belong, familiar village lanes gullywashed with new crumbling edges to them, a truncated wharf sloping down and in with slapping and sluicing water still threatening to detach more of it, some of the flotsam churning still and some already stranded, the breakers smashing on the headland rocks and climbing and flowering high with the characteristic rhythmic pause of deceleration at the crest of each watery explosion.

Well why, then?

There are meanings—perhaps to be understood in the ways in which we spoke obliquely and thought of those trips, impulsive and opportunistic as they were.

To get down there and see what had happened is a kind of allowable concern for something outside our own territory. Some exception can be made for the cottage at Towle's Cove belonging to my uncle, which, after all, we had some kind of lateral right to make damage inventory of. "Ed, we had a look at your place and everything seems okay. We couldn't locate your wooden lawnchairs though." Viewing wreckage, however, is seeing the new arrangements with the holes of "what has gone"—new gougings of skyspace in a treeline, Marlin's place without a fence around it any more, the cove beach now angled more steeply, some of its familiar flat places no longer there. Wreckage is loss, but it is the rearrangements too — and the scars that will be the new landmarks.

From beachcombing to salvaging to bird watching there are all kinds of finding: "After a hurricane at sea it is sometimes possible to observe the exotic tropical specimen blown thousands of miles from its normal range," though, true enough, the plumage may be in terrible shape. Uncle Ed has a two-thirds portion of a strangely-carved headboard from a far-travelling bed now attached to one of the inside walls of his cottage. Picking up afterwards is cleaning up and discovering. As one kicks the thing with his toe he thinks to himself, "Who the Hell do you suppose ever belonged to that?"

Still roaring. The day after, the breezes are still stiff and the seas big. Being near that stirs both mind and body somehow. There you have reason enough. Something seductive.

When I was a young man, my friends and I loved to fly kites, though we were no good at constructing them, nor did we understand the simplest principles of aerodynamics. In fact, a forty-mile trip to the shore was based on the premise, made by such coarse and graceless people as we were, that the stiffer the breeze, the better chance we had of success. At the headland above Towle's Cove we always could get one up, fly our poor kites. In that breezy place our kites flew. Kites were an excuse for a trip, sure. But a trip could also be an excuse for flying kites. You must remember that I was young, seventeen I think, and purpose and motive at that age are not what they have to be for the mature man.

2. What Was in the Trunk of the Blue Sedan and What It May Have Meant

This is the story of the time I planned and nearly executed a wonderful trip to the shore with a lovely girl named Yvonne Biron but ended instead in a pinegrove only halfway to the sea. In some ways it is a hard story to tell, partly because, after all these years, it can still embarrass me, and partly too, because I am trying to understand and account for the quality of onward-driving motive, especially as it can be so floweringly vague, compounded as it is of both careful plans and honest bewilderment as to what really will happen next. Take the matter of seduction, which in some not wholly literal way, I must have had in mind. Lodged in my watch pocket was the bright, shiny, duplicate tagged key for Uncle Ed's cottage. "Why don't I take the car tomorrow and run down to see how Uncle Ed's place made out." This simple sentence, a thrust at what I figured was not a very good chance, paid off. So too did the phone call to Yvonne, that excruciatingly desirable female I had so far only joked with at school in the deceptively pally way that young men like me considered appropriate for openers. "Hey Byron," I said into the dark phone — Byron was my pally name for her, making her laugh, and her laughing meant that I amused her, did it not? "Hey Byron, why don't you let me take you out somewhere tomorrow?"

"Sure, why not. I'll see what Grandmère says."

"Who?"

Yvonne just laughed.

When I told her nine, she assumed PM when I had meant AM. I wasn't doing badly, full of surprises — the unexpected — and that innocent hour seemed to work on Grandmère as well, though I didn't really follow the discussion I could hear off-phone in French.

"Grandmère's English is no good," said Yvonne, "but she knows who *you* are."

She emphasized the "you" just enough to make me wonder what was implied.

"Well, we can ride around and I'll show you some places I know about, okay?"

"Okay."

"Nine in the morning, Byron. You be up and ready."

Now comes the time to tell about the contents of the cartrunk — what I had surreptitiously put there in anticipation of a late August day with Yvonne by the stirring turbulent sea. I will itemize and probably lose my way denying simplicity of meanings: one basket of sandwiches, all chicken sandwiches which I had prepared myself by slicing lovely, long, slim white chunks of meat and placing them carefully on buttered salt and peppered de-crusted slabs of white bread; one galvanized scrub bucket full of hunks of ice, in which there sat at a rakish angle, a bottle of wine—where I got the wine I am still too embarrassed to recall with clarity—one picnic blanket; and, finally, a magnificent item overspreading all in that roomy trunk—a large, deepblue kite of my own inept design along with a remarkably big cone of tough binding thread of the kind used at the cotton mills. Upon this kite I had pasted in huge, cutout, orange block letters: Y-V-O-N-N-E.

You already know that the kite never flew, and the bright key to Uncle Ed's cottage never emerged from my little watch pocket, that the day ended in a pinegrove and not in the land of dreams come true. So why be in a hurry to leave these vague plans, objectified and waiting there in their dark enclosures (watch pocket, cartrunk) only to get to the pinegrove in the end? The pinegrove isn't much I can promise you. But I can perceive in the sandwiches, and in the wine for sipping there on the sunstreaming windy headland, a wonderful blossoming of unpredictable elegance: my plan, I think. And, in the blue over blue, the blue kite bouncing and bucking the bold orange announcement of my truly stricken ardour for Yvonne—markedly not Byron anymore, you see. The transition to Yvonne would properly take place in a setting of unmistakably stirring and moving, recently ravaged, land and seascape.

Do you think I wished to combine, with my ersatz champagne bucket and foolish kite, some kind of balancing loveliness between coltish playing and sophisticated advance? Well, I think so, or rather I think of how many meanings I may have meant and that would be one of them. Byron would have laughed at me. Yvonne, fed upon pure, classic chicken sandwiches would have laughed with me—and, to be honest about it, the bright key to the cottage, and what that may have implied, was too far along toward ends in my mind then, and still is now. If it had not been for the nemesis on the road, I think I would have lost ends in means anyhow — as I still often do — and, with that kite tugging suggestively in our joined hands, have come to wordy declaration rather than any kind of action. I still think lovely little Yvonne was worth that kind of delaying, courtly foolishness which I had to give. Besides, she said Grandmère knew who I was. Besides, I never quite knew what Yvonne might say or do next herself, come to think of it. She was as full of unpredictability as I was. Seduction? Simplicity of motive? Never! Forms and pictures, some of them dark and some of them bright.

3. A Beginning and a Conversation upon the Road

At nine o'clock, with the sun streaming on me and making me sweat already, I plugged up four flights of outside stairs to the top floor where Yvonne lived. As I ducked laundry and met the inquisitive stares of kids and their mothers, my mind was on Grandmère more than on Yvonne. "She knows who you are" stuck in my mind and I was beginning to think that maybe I could fathom something from her manner, even enduring the awkwardness of English and French, of youth and elder (a lot elder as I imagined it), of translation and introduction. When Yvonne slipped out of the door onto the landing to meet me, I felt cheated.

"Grandmère?" I asked.

"Store," she said, tilting her head to indicate that we should descend the stairs and leave and why not right then. And, why not, though I had a feeling that if I could have looked at Grandmère eye to eye I might have learned something. Her eyes would say more saying, "I know who you are," certainly, than Yvonne's did glancing over into mine as we went down. All I could read from them, as she lightly brushed my forearm with her fingertips, was mischief—of which I might be companionable sharer or victim, or both.

"Grandmère says you are a good boy," Yvonne giggled.

"How does she know that?"

"Then you admit it," she replied, running ahead and jumping into the car.

"What makes you think you got the right car?" I asked when I caught up to her.

"You're getting in, aren't you?" was all she said.

Then looking over at her I remember I noticed her white shorts—and tanned legs—probably avoiding her eyes led me to gaze elsewhere than into such direct confusion. The control. The control was the deep blue and electric orange assertion hidden away in the trunk for later on. Well then, in the meantime conversation proceeded and ebbed in such manner as implied that the present is merely to be squandered. The following must surely be a true sample:

"Where are we going, Buddy?"

"That's what you'd like to know and I'm not about to tell."

"Why won't you tell me…. Just tell me what *kind* of place it is."

"It's just a little place I know of."

"It's some place you're afraid I won't go to if I know."

"Maybe."

"Oh Buddy, come on, I'm going with you whether I want to or not, aren't I? Can't you tell me yet?"

"No."

"Why not?"

"Maybe it's what you said; you wouldn't be going if you knew where it is we're going. Yes, that's it, you said it already, I guess. If you knew where we're going, you probably wouldn't go."

We were passing a field of cows, half of them standing, half of them prone in the green cool of the bright August morning.

"How do you know?" Byron said at last—had she been listening to the hum of the tires or watching the cows? "Maybe I would, maybe I'd be glad to, maybe I could even think of some better place."

"Like where?"

"What do you mean?"

"Where would be a better place than where I'm taking us—if you can think of some place better?"

"I can't say that till I know where you're taking me and what for."

"Well what do you think I'm taking you someplace for?" I came down hard on the "you"—perhaps like the "you" of Byron's Grandmère, as Byron had translated for me.

"How do I know that? Shouldn't you tell me?"

"You must have some idea, Byron, if you can think of a better place."

"Well I don't."

We seemed to be passing an endless field of sweet corn.

"But can't you just tell me what you think is a better place? Look, you must be thinking of something. Maybe you're thinking what I'm thinking."

"What's that?"

"Come on, Byron, just tell me, okay?"

"Tell you what?"

"Forget it."

"God, there's Teddy!" she shrieked suddenly. "That was Teddy," she said, pivoting round quickly and looking back through the rear window. "Stop, Buddy, that was Teddy!"

4. The Nemesis on the Road

I see Teddy best in my mind's eye as he trudges the highway alone—that is, before Yvonne and I happen along and find him hitchhiking at the far end of a field of tall-tasseled August sweetcorn fifteen miles out of town. In the bright morning, squatbrowed Teddy, a veering hulking lad, negotiates the roadedge uncertainly. At times he waves at passing cars with an unreadable sweep of his arm and at other times ignores the traffic, sucking and blowing on his ever-present mouth organ. Over his shoulder he carries a bundle tied to a stout stick, in a manner I have seen nowhere else but in the funny-papers. He seems for all his stumbling handicaps and dithering movement to be resolute after his own manner. Teddy is going somewhere.

If I did not know Teddy from school — a familiar figure there, dwelling more in corridor than in classroom with the indulgence of the principal, who allowed him a statusless, ungraded existence so long as he didn't wail on his harmonica when classes were in session — I would have thought him fearsome, a witless six-foot, 200-pound, rootless hobo, the kind to terrify farm wives and smash the skulls of barking farmdogs with his club. Though he drooled a bit and had a wild look in his eye, he was harmless. I always figured I was kinder to him than most because I would poke him in the belly with my finger and say, "Blow me 'Stardust,' Teddy. Come on now, I'm sick of 'Deep Purple'." Secretly I suspected that he had addled his brains, drained them of energy and usefulness, by his perpetual sucking and blowing, maybe denying his grey matter needed oxygen.

It was another mile before Byron could convince me that she really meant what she was saying and I pulled the car to the side of the road.

"We've got to pick him up, Buddy. He's hitching. God, that Teddy!"

"Why? Byron, why in Hell pick him up?" I emphasized the "him" considerably. I was prepared, I thought, for the unexpected, for mischief, for alteration of my own foolish plan-after all, I never had to open the trunk, never actually release my moony message to the light of day, let alone to the skies on the blue salty air — but this request seemed grotesque. Christ, was this some idea of hers of fun?

There was no mistaking Byron's seriousness, though. She reached over and clutched my shoulder — I could feel the strength in her small hand as she did so. "He's running away," she said. "God, we've got to get him home."

"So why should I care?" I said. "What for?"

I had to live another ten years at least before I was no longer so stupid as not to see that what she said next was hard for her. "He's running away, Buddy. You've got to help me. God, that Teddy's my uncle. Didn't you know that?"

I simply sat, trying to accommodate such a piece of news.

"Please," she said.

Finally I thought of something to say, and that probably helped me back to action and I began turning the car around in a farmhouse driveway.

"Your uncle?" Did I try to make myself sound unshocked? I can't truly remember.

"How old is he?"

"Seventeen," she said, as we began to scan the roadside for the place where we had spotted him a few minutes earlier.

5. The Great Pretenders and the Game They Play

Even before we came abreast of Teddy, Byron had rolled down the window on her side and with her head out was letting fly with an angry blast like a mother scolding a naughty kid. I hadn't even known that Teddy was French, his speech was usually so giggly and slurred, but there was no mistaking his understanding now. He was grim and petulant as he walked on past the car. My choice then was to back down the highway on Byron's open window side or to turn around again. I did the latter, and now Teddy was on my side of the car and it was my turn. I would try him in English in a calmer, friendlier way, banking on my record as a good-guy joker.

"Hey, Sport," I called. "Where are you goin'?" Teddy ignored me and lurched onward.

"Come on, Teddy, blow me 'Stardust', okay?"

He never looked over but stuck the harmonica into his mouth, producing a single uuurgh-aaarghuuurgh sound and then immediately put it back into his shirt pocket. I took this as recognition of who I was. Two cars shot past us in the left lane between Teddy and us.

"Hey!" I yelled, trying to see into the rearview mirror while I was only vaguely aware of Byron crowding up to me on the right—practically into my lap. "You can come with us. What do you say?"

"Teddy does what he wants unless you get tough," Yvonne said. "We have to."

The two of us were cheek to cheek peering out at him. It was hopeless trying to see into the mirror, but I tried because I was worried that we might be rammed from behind, we were creeping along so slowly.

"Tell him Grandmère will use the switch." I could smell her sweet, lovely breath, but I was thinking about what she said. "You tell him, Buddy. Tell him you've got the switch here—no," she clutched my hand this time. "No, he needs to see it, don't tell him that."

"Just say, 'the switch,'" she said after a while. "See what he does."

"The switch, Teddy," I yelled—"the switch!"

Teddy kept moving, eyes ahead.

"Switch, in English? How about in French?"

"We always just tell him 'switch.' He knows we don't have it with us."

Yvonne then scrambled back to her side of the seat and pointed up ahead to the left where a dusty farm road met the highway at the end of the cornfield. Teddy would soon cross it.

"Pull in there," she commanded. "We can cut him off."

I made a left turn and in a cloud of dust intersected Teddy's line of advance about five feet in front of him. As the car jerked to a halt, I heard an angry blasting horn from a transport roaring past us. God, I'd failed to signal, that's for sure. Could have killed us. Yvonne jumped over to my side again and resumed her scolding, her head out the window once more. We had Teddy stopped now, and Yvonne's quick tongue was keeping him rooted in his tracks: Whatever she was saying to him, it gradually became softer and gentler. Her left knee was grinding painfully into my groin. Finally Teddy moved. He took the stick and bandanna off his shoulder and let it trail onto the ground.

His large, lumpy face began to break up, and soon he was sobbing loudly and gasping out some long story to Yvonne.

"What's he saying?"

"Quiet," Yvonne snapped, flicking her left hand, the back of it, in my direction.

Then suddenly Teddy approached, opened the back door of the car, threw in his stick and climbed in after. He was grinning through his tears.

"Welcome aboard, Teddy," I said. "Where to, Sport?"

"No," Yvonne said, for no good reason that I could see.

"'ollywood," grinned Teddy, pulling out the mouth organ from his shirt pocket.

Before he could begin blowing on it, though, he started up his bawling again—a sudden loud and angry wail. I had been in the process of backing out of the farm road onto the highway and turning the car toward home.

"The other way, Buddy. You're going the wrong way!" Yvonne cried.

"Where then?"

"'ollywood," Teddy said, now that I was turning the car around, away from home.

Yvonne interrupted. "He's running off to Hollywood to be in the movies, Buddy. He wants to play his mouth organ for a talent scout."

Teddy was happy again, sprawling in the back seat. He whipped out his harmonica and the terrible sounds began: uuurgh-aaargh-uuurgh-uuurghaaargh-uuurgh-aaargh.

As soon as I began to speak, Teddy stopped the racket and leaned forward. "Hollywood is three thousand…" but I broke off my protest when I saw the disgusted look on Yvonne's face, as if to say how stupid I was not even to see the point of this absolutely necessary, even crucial lie.

I couldn't think of anything else to say. Teddy leaned back again seeming to be satisfied that no more was going to be said and resumed his concert. Yvonne's head was turned away, looking out her side window. I simply drove along trying to think of something, but not succeeding. Teddy's harmonica was incessant, though after a while I thought I heard an elegant variation or two: uurghy-uurghyaargh, urrghy-uurghy-aargh. But I worried that the crack in the rhythm might be in my own head. In a few miles we'd be coming to a turnoff to the coast, the main highway continuing south. Teddy would spot that too if we turned onto it, I thought. So much for Towle's Cove today.

Yvonne suddenly turned around in her seat and rummaged in her bag. She must have come up with an idea. I could see she was attempting to appear casual, even when she opened the glove compartment and searched in there. I thought she may have wanted a road map in order to plan a roundabout, unfamiliar way home, but I was wrong. She pulled out a Kleenex box from the compartment and a lipstick from her bag. Spreading out several of the tissues she began writing — a message! To Teddy her head and shoulders would have given no clue what she was doing. When she finished she laid four tissues side by side on the seat and then doubling up her small hand into a fist rapped my leg, almost formally, like someone knocking shyly on a door. As I glanced down to read what she had written, she spun around and kneeled on the seat like a small child as she faced her Uncle Teddy in the back seat. The music stopped and the two of them began conversing rapidly. I read the message scrawled in smeary red and then immediately balled up the Kleenex and stuffed them into my pocket. It said:

HAD TO SAY WERE RUNNING OFF ALSO TO GET MARRIED GOT IT?

"Okay," I said, nodding once, my eyes on the road ahead. I assumed she heard and saw, though she hadn't faced toward me in some little while. In a few minutes she was back jotting another message. This one said simply, I'M SORRY. Now our eyes met and I was astonished to notice that she had been crying, and as we looked at each other quizzically and probably stupidly, I noticed that more tears were coming.

"Yvonne," I said, "you're running away with me, you've got to sit here and not way over there," and I gestured to the seat near me. "It's not proper if you don't." We both tried to smile, her attempt producing a sniffle and mine a strange gulp, but she snuggled up to me in a passable imitation of a moonstruck eloping lover, and I drove with only my left hand on the wheel.

"I probably shouldn't," she said. "I ought to be mad with you."

I was too pleased with my own remark to wonder why, and I decided to delay for a while thinking about what we'd do with Teddy. He was still serenading us, uuurgh-aaargh-uuurgh, as we sped on and past the turnoff to the coast.

"Where was it you were taking me?" she asked.

"That's for me to know and you to ask"—a stupid thing to say, I know, but I was too peaceful and exhausted to think of anything else.

6. The Pinegrove Where the Story Ends

Well, what do you think? We grew hungry as noon approached, and I had a couple of choices. With two mouths to feed not counting my own, there was the lunch in the trunk. But Teddy and the wine together was something I didn't want to think about, though I did all the same; I couldn't help it. Maybe he would just as soon suck on a lump of ice—no, not really. Besides, to expose the secret of the kite—the kite without the context was a foolish thing for sure: no sea nor no sky where foolishness might not be for sure at all, but instead a form and picture of brightness. No, it had to be a pinegrove at last where a hamburger stand, a good one though, nestled under high-crowned, ancient trees. Picnic tables were generously dispersed through the grove where customers could drive up next to them. That's what I did, drove in there thinking that I needn't open the trunk at all, and we stepped out onto the soft needly floor near a table as far away from the stand and other picnickers as possible.

This story ends in a pinegrove, and as we sat at the picnic table together I began inventing in my own mind all the ways that the story must not, could not, end. Opening the trunk was out: because (a) to let Teddy fly the kite in the pasture across the road would involve me in too much simultaneous explanation and action. But he did need diversion; I caught a clue from Yvonne that delay, right here in the pinegrove, was what she wanted. And (b) when neither was looking to bust and crumple the kite, hide the wine in the blanket, and rescue the sandwiches. I had my chance for that when Yvonne insisted I stay with Teddy while she went for hamburgers, but I was watching her every motion (desecrate the kite in such a melodramatic way? Never!) seeing her not only approach the stand but going around back and out of sight and then staying a good while there. "Aha!" I thought to myself, not at all understanding why. No other customers were entering, just using the little window in the front to place their orders.

"'ollywood," Teddy said, grinning.

"'Stardust,'" I answered, very much in the spirit of the conversation. Uuurgh-aaargh-uuurgh.

Most of all I yearned for the story to end here in the pinegrove fairly soon and not four or five more hours down the road, with painful long-distance phone calls and explanations in two languages at nightfall. Though, maybe Teddy would fall to sleep then and we could head north again under the cover of gathering darkness.

But when Yvonne returned at last and we had eaten our hamburgers, a strange peace descended on us. Yvonne nodded at me and smiled. "It's okay," she said, leaning back against a grandfather pine and stretching her pretty legs out before her on the rusty, needly floor. Teddy sat at the picnic table with his elbows on it and sucked and blew his uurghaaargh-uuuurghs in a dreamier, softer way. I sat sideways on the passenger side of the front seat of the car, with the door flung open and with my feet on the good ground. I picked out the balled Kleenex from my pocket and idly read Yvonne's scrawled message, though I didn't need to — I knew what it said by heart. The few rays of sun filtering through the pines were beginning to show a late afternoon slant. Seabreezes and headlands were far, far away.

I smelled not stirring salt air but somnolent summerbaked pine needles. Uncle Ed's cottage; Uncle Teddy's concert in the grove. Why were none of us moving and taking the next step? Planning? I longed for Teddy's music to make him so drowsy that I could ask Yvonne directly, "What next?" but it was her eyes, not his, which were closing. Was she asleep? Teddy began to stir with signs of restlessness. He spoke to Yvonne who translated for me without opening her eyes.

"He has to go to the bathroom, Buddy."

"How and what," I began thinking, when she added, "Out behind the stand. We just have to show him the door."

When we returned Teddy headed for the car, as if he expected us to follow and get in after him, but Yvonne; eyes open, spoke to him sharply. "No more today, Teddy," she said winking at me. "We'll camp here tonight."

The wink was to keep me playing the game, sure. I was so dense I had to be given the signals unmistakably. What she said in English was for both Teddy and me simultaneously, for the idiot and for the idiotic. That was annoying, but I also liked her little fiction, "camp here for the night." I only hoped she liked the game a little too. Was she saying anything else?

Teddy acquiesced without question and sprawled on the ground, his music temporarily stilled. I made a little campfire of twigs, playing the game for Teddy's benefit, I supposed, and he and I hunched together at it as he poked it with a stick and I stared into the tiny flames. After a time a question took shape in my mind: when Yvonne had taken so long getting the hamburgers, when I had taken Teddy over to the bathroom. Out behind the stand—a phonebooth. I remembered seeing it. I had to ask Yvonne.

I therefore stationed myself behind Teddy where he couldn't see me, catching Yvonne's eye. I mimed the question, pointing to her, then to the distant hamburger stand, and then did an elaborate silent imitation of someone phoning, complete with gestures of dropping coins into slots. And then I pointed back to her again and assumed an exaggerated questioning expression. She laughed heartily (I probably looked desperate and foolish), and Teddy looked around at me, but too late to notice anything.

She nodded yes in answering exaggeration — to my question obviously, but she also said, "Yes, Teddy likes our camp don't you, Teddy? Buddy made us a nice fire."

Teddy answered in French this time, as it turned out, to request another hamburger.

As the three of us made our way through a second round of lunch there was ample time to ponder. I knew now that someone was coming to the rescue, but who? And how would it be managed? I partially took ease from Yvonne's tranquillity until I thought "Grandmère knows who you are." No, there seemed no possibility in that. The police? Well, maybe so. Who was Teddy's usual keeper? Grandmère?

Several times I tried to sit near enough to Yvonne to murmur, whisper, or even mouth my question, "Who's coming?" But whenever I got anywhere near her as she sat at the bench or lolled against her tree, Teddy approached, staring directly at us, smiling a happy drooly smile, and soon he'd be pulling at my arm wanting me to gather more sticks for the fire with him. He showed no interest in doing so by himself. It was clear to me that Teddy was beginning to think of me as his best pal — source of fun, source of food, and most of all, means of flight.

"Camp," he said, grinning even wider.

"Blow us some more 'Deep Purple,' Teddy," I said, and when he began I tried snuggling up to Yvonne, who was reclining against her tree facing the highway, scanning it through the pines. Teddy's eyes were riveted on the two of us as he sucked and blew, and I figured, correctly, that he would interpret my movement with benign approval. I nuzzled Yvonne's ear as she remained immobile and even stiff, and then I whispered — too loudly — in her ear, "Who's coming?"

In a flash she recoiled, scowled, grabbed a hunk of my hair and pulled my head forward, blew painfully in my ear, and then pulling me closer to her again, breathed the answer sweetly, "Paul."

"Who's that?" We were partly wrestling, partly embracing.

"My cousin." She just barely managed her reply as the sounds from the mouth organ stopped and Teddy was looming over us and pulling my shirtsleeve and grinning.

"Sticks for the fire," he said for the tenth time that afternoon.

As we foraged together for yet another load of twigs and dead pine branches, Yvonne called after, "So what, Buddy?"

I looked back; she was smiling, maybe even laughing.

The end came suddenly, though I don't know to this day whether or not to say brutally. Everything happened too quickly. Yvonne must have seen them first, then Teddy, because I heard his loud wailing cry and the roaring motor of the red panel truck and its screeching brakes as it halted right behind my car almost simultaneously. Teddy was up and running as Paul and two other young men—all about my age and one of them carrying a coil of stout rope—bounded after him and tackled him a few feet from the campfire. I was aware only of shouts I could not comprehend, a kicking, thrashing struggle, and a trussed and writhing Teddy being loaded into the back of the truck. He was frothing at the mouth. In a moment they were gone—all of them: Paul and his two friends, Teddy and Yvonne, and I had the pinegrove, my kite and elegant picnic, the campfire, and the oncoming evening all to myself.

I doused the fire with the melted water from my ice bucket; but no, I neither burned the beautiful blue and orange kite, wistfully gazing at the smoke winding up through the treetops, nor quaffed the warm wine, flinging the empty bottle aside, a coarser and wiser drunken young man. As I drove my long way home, though, in twilight and then in darkness, I was thoughtful, wondering what things meant. I reconstructed scenes and pondered the few words said to me, just a very few words of English, amid the wild concluding scene in the grove. Yvonne had only the chance to say, "Call me up" as she was hustled into the back of the truck with the struggling Teddy. Paul made her do that, explaining to me the best he could, "She has to talk to him going home, okay?" Paul's friends, or maybe relatives, must have been having trouble holding him because I could hear thumping and clunking, probably Teddy's boots against the inside of the truck. Before he jumped in behind the wheel, Paul stopped and punched me playfully on the shoulder with his fist. "Thanks kid," he said. I don't recall my reply.

What I remembered most though, going over it again and again in my mind was the incomprehensible moment when Teddy, just before he was dumped into the bed of the truck, sprung one of his arms free and pointed first to me and then to Yvonne, shouting indignantly — something. Whatever it was, no one had time or inclination to translate, but it caused everyone to laugh and grin, looking my way. Yvonne answered something back, making the boys laugh again, even while they caught Teddy's arm and roped it again to his body.

I did call Yvonne up. The next day.

"Where were you taking me, Buddy?" she asked.

I told her. Reduced to words I described the kite, the headland above Towle's Cove, the elegant picnic fare — even elaborating on that, as I am capable of doing.

She paused a long while before responding.

"That would have been nice, Buddy," she said at last.

She paused again.

"Buddy?"

"Yes?"

"That would have been nice, I said."

"I know — I heard you."

"You are a funny one, Buddy."

"I'll be seeing you at school," I replied.

Fern

I first wrote about Fern some 30 years ago in a childish but sensational essay I prepared as the result of a school assignment. In a way, I've never since completely lost the feeling of what utter artistic and popular success can be, and I can date from that performance the start of certain of my powerful longings toward such an end. The triumph really was sensational, or so it seems to me looking back at it now. Miss Tarnish more than once exclaimed over the originality I had shown in choosing for my favourite pet one dead long before I had been born, as she and my schoolmates listened engrossed to tale after tale of Fern's boundless good nature, sense of humour, loyalty, compassion and all-round massive nobility.

When I told them how Fern had been killed at last by a trolley on Pine Street, the toughest boys in the class sincerely wept, as I was doing too, though my weeping was not untainted with certain joys of discovery. I remember as well, and I put it down as a kind of confession, that when my written essay was completely read through—not all that long, really, perhaps four pages of foolscap—I spoke on without interruption, laying the essay by on the table before me, while I woke the sleeping forms of the dead to walk about with us for a time in that little schoolroom. Miss Tarnish made no notice of the transition, nor did I, really, though in the midst of the story of Fern with the cream bottles and the crippled child, I remember thinking on Joan Martin's feeble and shy account of her rabbit: "How Daddy and the children laugh to see him twitch his funny pink nose." I felt a kind of pity for such as the Martins, clustered about and chuckling at a creature so minimal as a bunny, while I, with every one's heartfelt and manifest approbation, was evoking an heroic age indeed. To me, I must confess, my own imagination seemed as massive as Fern's great shaggy form and my tongue as expressive as her fathomless, brown loving eyes. I did not care, or perhaps did not even notice, that the Martins' pitiable loving—no doubt even on the very day of little Joan's nearly inarticulate testimony — was of quivering, live, pink flesh, whereas mine, so moving and so magical, was of a creature of clouds.

So it was I merely retailed stories I had heard from my family; so it was I learned without ever having to think about it, of the superiority of the vision over the fleshly fact. Miss Tarnish and her little charges, all my people now in this story, even little Joan, her father and her bunny, taught me that.

"No, it was quite common in those days," said Uncle Wallace, pulling at his out-sized, drooping pipe and blowing a bluish plume toward the ceiling. "Fern was exceptionally intelligent and probably the best of her type, but many families relied on their dogs to look after their youngsters in those days, you remember that. It's a long while since I've seen one responsible at all. Maybe it's that folks have forgotten how to trust them."

"But you knew you could trust her just by looking at her." Zoe's brown eyes, sad and faraway, gave credence to the idea that long ago unspoken sympathies must have existed between herself and the redoubtable Fern. She still mourned the sudden death of goodness on Pine Street over 40 years ago. Didn't we all.

They were all there — there in an oval frame on the piano: Wallace, Edward, Zoe and Zena, my mother, Margaret — she ran away and married my father, you know, not a month after Fern was killed by the trolley — and little Edna, who ran away too, for complex but similar reasons, but what she did is still a cross to bear — still. In front, proprietary and maternal, not without a hint of allowable merriment in her eyes, sprawled the huge Fern, body lounging at its ease, head erect, alert and unquestionably intelligent. All of them inhabit the sepia atmosphere of the old photograph. With strangely appropriate irony, not lost on a boy like me, the image of little Edna was mottled, undoubtedly because of the imperfect art of photography in those earlier days, though the accident, if that is what it was, struck me as a portent, and now that Edna resided out West as a kind of exile in her shame, I wondered if others felt as I did, a bit awed in the face of strange correspondendences.

"Your mother used to pull her hair something terrible," Zoe said, "and Fern was so patient and understanding with her; she always felt anguish over it when she grew older. 'Poor thing,' she used to say, 'how could I have done that?' when we'd tell her about it."

Sad-eyed Zoe, who claimed, as they all did in their own ways, to have been closest to Fern, still lived. My mother, the hair-puller and the guiltstruck, had died two years before.

"Do you remember how Fern used to look after little Edna?" Wallace resumed, letting go with another blue cloud. "Why every time she'd try to put on a dirty frock or stockings Fern would yank on those clothes with her teeth and bother her till she'd have to go ask mother for something fresh. It was Fern kept up the dignity of the family in those days, not mother, God rest her soul. What was it? Forty years ago she went at last?"

"A year before Fern got hit by the trolley, and I'll never forget that to save me," Zoe said, "then Margaret went away and then Edna."

"You know, boy," Wallace said, turning to me. "There never was a dog like Fern before and never will be again. Did we ever tell you about the little crippled Ames girl and how Fern brought her the cream?"

I had, a thousand times, but would one not ask again to hear how Fern, in the early morning before anyone in town but the milkman was awake, had for a whole summer filched a half-pint of cream every day from the back porch of our house and brought it a half-mile to the little house of the widow Ames? The doctors said afterward it was just what that little mite of a girl needed to pull her through that bad summer. The widow, you know, didn't have any idea who was leaving the cream, but at any rate it was the only food that little Annie would take, so she was grateful and gave it to her every day just like clockwork.

"Isn't it true, Uncle Wallace, that in those days they didn't understand vitamins and that sort of thing?"

"You're right there, my boy; all the doctors knew then was that poor little Annie had to eat something, just to keep her alive."

"But Fern knew, somehow, what she needed, right?"

"She certainly seemed to, though God knows how," Zoe said, sighing. "It certainly gives you pause to think."

"Yes sir, Old Doc Tuttle could vouch for the story if he were alive today. He said he'd never seen anything like it. Nobody else had, of course, either."

"God's will."

"Yes, if you like, God's will."

"There was something religious about that dog, you can't deny it."

"No, I don't deny it, Zoe, I remember as well as you do how she used to go after Catholics. How she could tell the difference I don't know, but she sure could."

"She'd never hurt a soul, now; you wouldn't want the boy to think she would."

"No, no, but wouldn't she terrify them though. You remember how she got that Father Flynn so he'd barely come out onto the street at all."

Now why is it, you may well ask, that a man like myself, grown to sober and rational middle age, with all those people of his childhood — the possible exception being Edna in California — dead and gone, would resurrect such of their follies as to provoke ridicule to fall upon their departed spirits? It is not merely that having told stories of Fern once before I found myself a spellbinder for a brief hour and crave repetition. I should like to make a distinction. What I wish to contemplate is the power, not in myself but in Fern as she came alive in the stories I told. Was it my own belief, shining out and leaping into other beings, that softened the hearts of the toughest of seventh-grade urchins? For a believer I was then, and am not a believer now. Yet I must say there is an oddity in myself; I don't doubt it and that is working in me too. It makes me still worship, for that's what I do — worship indeed — the memory of other people's memory — of that accursed dog.

I have on my desk the photograph. No oddity is discernible in that, for here is a shrine and memento of my mother and her brothers and sisters, my people of the Worcester branch of the family—the most illustrious ones. But there too is Fern. If I honour them must I not honour as well their most persistent article of faith, namely, that for some reason connected with the fate of the whole Worcester family—all its virtues and honour and character—all that made life good and meaningful became lodged in the soul of that huge, faithful, family pet, and that "worth," as it used to be known, was erased suddenly from the face of the earth forever on a June morning on Pine Street in 1925. How much do I have a share in such things, I ask myself. There are times when I begin to think but little. Sooner or later, however, an event will conspire to rouse the Worcester blood in me over against that of the Hart—my father's branch, for I am Ernest Hart Jr.

It was only yesterday when by way of business Annie Ames came to my office—she consults me concerning her estate—and gazed at the photograph. What she said still buzzes in my Worcester ears.

"Oh poor Fern," she said, lightly touching the glass with her crooked finger. "People today would never believe what a saint she was, eh, Mr. Hart? Nothing has ever seemed so happy or so good in the world since that awful trolley had to go and kill her, poor thing."

How the old people love the same stories, the ones they tell over and over again! Do they simply forget that they have told them before or do they find their chosen anecdotes as representative of the few nuggets of truth that are worth saving in the dross of a lifetime? In my town, Fern, St. Fern, I suppose, figured in most of such stories the old folks tell, and are forever surfacing just when I begin to think I am a rational arid balanced human being inhabiting the nineteen-seventies.

Carlton Nixon, for instance, a butcher now retired for twenty years or more. What does this morose little man almost green with grey age invariably say when he hobbles up to see me at every church supper or lodge meeting I attend? "Ah yes, you're the Worcester grandson, aren't you? Margaret's boy—yes, Margaret's boy.

Married one of the Harts who used to run the ice-cream parlours. You know there's something about your grandfather I'll never forget, and I'll tell you what it is—that dog of his, a St. Bernard maybe, but not all St. Bernard, no sir, something else as well mixed in there. You wouldn't remember because it was before your time." (Oh the irony of it! How well I do remember, but all my life I was the too late born and was not allowed to remember in fact; I missed the Golden Age by three and a half years and have been thrashing about in the debased present ever since I can remember.)

"Well, that dog, it had an odd name, like a girl's name, you know. Fern, yes, that's it, Fern. I suppose your folks might have told you about her. Well that dog used to come into my shop with your grandfather—acted like a perfect lady even though she was as big as a barn and you know the old gentleman just idolized that dog. When times was good he used to buy her expensive cuts of meat. Indulging her, you might say. Nobody did that kind of thing in them days, though they do now more than you might think now that times seem good for everybody.

"Well, the very week old Worcester lost his fortune—I guess I don't need to tell you about that, eh? You'd be a rich man today if it wasn't for that—well, old Tom Worcester ordered up a couple of steaks for that dog just like nothing had happened at all, and when I began to wrap 'em up she commenced to growl and bark. We tried giving her the steak but that just made it worse, and you know we couldn't hush that dog till I went and got a bucket of scraps—the kind we used to give away—Willis Fox would vouch for what I say if he weren't dead and gone—well that dog—no doubt about it—knew something had gone wrong at home and wasn't going to be no luxury and burden on the family. There's no other way to explain it. Well, if old Worcester left you anything—I don't know if he did or not—you might say you owe it to that remarkable dog. What do you say to that? Eh? What do you say to that?"

So it is I owe my legacy, 100 dollars, two ten-dollar gold pieces, and a gold railroad watch not to the love of Grandfather Worcester, who did, I think, regard me as a nuisance and surely as an unfortunate occurrence, but to the sacrificial domestic economy of the great Fern. I reveal, I suppose, that my feelings toward that looming figure are equivocal. Well, so they are.

I know, too, how many another feels, and those feelings are not always benign. I know that the reputation of Fern of the Worcesters redounds upon me whether I like it or not, and sometimes that is agreeable to me and sometimes it isn't. I can't forget what Denny Poole said to me once when I was much younger—younger and spunkier. There I had come upon him outside his shack, drunk as he usually was, lacing the hide of his little terrier with a coach whip. He was a sorry sight, red-eyed and vengeful, and the poor cur was howling with pain. I, the protector of the weak, determined to front Denny, a known terror, and after summoning courage told him he should be ashamed of himself for so molesting the poor brute. I would settle his hash but good if he did not desist and furthermore I would report him to the authorities. The bluff worked, mostly because I was bigger and younger I suppose, and he let the whip sag in his hand while the mutt scurried under the porch.

"Now the bastard won't be coming out for a week—just after dark when I can't catch him," Denny said.

Then as if he had thought of something—maybe he recognized just who I was for the first time—at any rate he made a violent but uncoordinated attempt to crack his whip more or less in my direction, and gulping and sobbing and thick-tongued shouted at me what I know I didn't misunderstand. "God damn it all to Hell, you're the Worcester kid—a Worcester for Christ sake—tells me not to whip my li'l dog! Don't I know how Tom Worcester trained that damned polar bear he called a dog!"

He let out a roar and lashed the sagging stair rail with a roundhouse swing. "A Worcester tells me how to handle a dog. That's a Goddamned laugh. I wouldn't treat no dog like he did even if I am ol' drunk Poole. You forgit too easy. There's plenty as can remember, don't forgit that!"

With that he was in the house, bumping around and howling God knows what while I stood in the road and reeled myself—as if I had heard the very name of Yahweh shouted in jesting lubricity through the corridors of a brothel. Forget that? Do you suppose that possible?

"Edward, of course, owed his life to Fern," Zoe said. "I guess you know that, Ernest."

I knew that well enough and came to associate Uncle Edward's demise in the bridge accident in far away Costa Rica with the fact that Fern was no longer alive to keep him from a watery death. Improbable and foolish, yes, to imagine that the great creature who had pulled little Edward gasping and blue from the swimming hole on Uncle Sim's farm, should have, if she had lived, accompanied that spruce young engineer, even granting the family's compliance, on his Central American adventure, and to imagine she could herself have survived the plummeting of that entire span into the boiling waters of the gorge to pull handsome Edward to safety a second time. But if you doubt that my mind could have so connected these events in such a way, then you fail to give credence to the force of Fern's memory among the Worcesters in the days of my youth. Never strong on logic and probabilities, the Worcesters, and I was one of them, took as a matter of course the idea that upon Fern's death nearly coincident with the financial ruin of the family and the rapid disintegration of what may only be called their luck, all experiences, all living underwent a sea-change into the fixed, perpetually disintegrating, minimally interesting and doleful present. Any one of them, Wallace, or Zoe, or Zena, or my mother, could, perhaps, have even articulated if they chose, but they chose not to, the degree to which feeling and thought about loss and aging and all the sad things of life came to be compressed into talk about Fern, as emotional shorthand, as euphemism if you like, as verbal artifice.

But consider myself, who came later, who was as a child naturally is, literal-minded, who in his pathetic wish to attach himself to the feelings of others, is an unquestioning believer—oh, as I believed in God as a kind of ghostly Grandfather Worcester tilting back on his heavenly chair and propping his feet upon the actual golden rails of heaven, so did I believe in Fern as a protean form of divine beneficence who larrapped through the actual world in the happier times which had preceded my being. For long into my adolescence it seemed more plausible that Fern should have performed miraculous feats of love than that they could in any way be doubted. Consider too, how I, resident of a fallen world, came to think of myself as virtually a symbol or an embodiment of it.

"Yes," Uncle Wallace said, not even yet with a voice untainted with envy, "she was in a way more Edward's dog than anyone else's."

Zoe's eyes, sadder and deeper than ever, expressed silent protest that such invidious distinctions be broached. How the fiery Zena, had she been present, would have challenged Wallace's acknowledgement, his realistic honesty, and precipitated the familiar discussion, Thomistic in its orderly marshalling of arguments on the minutest points, catechistic in the droning repetition of shared articles of belief which had to precede, as a matter of decency, variations of interpretation upon the single grand theme. But Zena, happily or unhappily was not there, and so it was that an entire colloquy was bypassed, though its quality and its terms, known to all, hovered in all minds as a known block of truth, serviceable for reference with a sigh or a nod.

"Edward, really, was the only one who could rough and tumble with her, you must admit that."

Wallace was unsparing of himself in this, for he, older than Edward and more "serious" as it was called then, had from the first gracefully acknowledged and cultivated Fern's dignity more than her other qualities.

I knew what was coming and dreaded it, so much did the conversation promise to turn upon what defined the very blood in my veins as tainted with that of the Goths and Vandals.

"Margaret's Ernest, now — that would be your father, son," Uncle Wallace said in tones that seemed at least to be avuncular; did I not know with excruciating precision to whom he referred?

"Back when he first started coming to the house courting Margaret" — here was that air of tolerant amusement that always accompanied references to my father's courtship — "he tried to make up to Fern the way Edward did, tried to roughhouse with her, but she wouldn't have any of it if you recall."

Zoe nodded. "Yes, you'd almost have thought Ernest Hart was a Catholic."

Wallace, checking Zoe's emotional penchant to rewrite history in terms of her simple desires, corrected her. "Oh not so much of that, Zoe; it really wasn't as open as all that. Besides, you have to remember how she tried to make it up to him when it began to be clear he was going to be one of the family, bringing him the evening paper first, for instance. Oh, I'd say Fern was reconciled even before Father."

Now I was not what you would call a precocious child, and remember I reverenced the memory of Fern with unquestioning intensity, but the patronizing quality of Fern's acceptance was not lost on me: After all, I, Ernest Hart Jr., bore my father's name and by that fact alone was implicated in the rebuff. My difficulty was that I also understood with my Worcester blood the full implications of Fern's gesture. The cheerful vulgarity of the act, like a cartoon dog fetching newspaper, pipe and slippers, seemed deliberately scaled to the understandings of the robust Ernest, son of the Harts who ran the ice-cream parlours and who came breezily unconcerned with the finer points of conduct to court, impelled as he was by the mating urge, the delicate Margaret Worcester in her castle.

Is it necessary to add that I, in the long imaginations of childhood, fancied myself as intimate with Fern as my elders had been — in happier moods frolicking with her in flowery fields more unrestrainedly than my Uncle Edward in his prime, in more pensive moments imagining her at the foot of my bed, guardian not merely against the thieves of the night who might invade the sanctuary of my nursery but also against those other-wordly devils of the spirit that glide unbidden into the mind of the wakeful child? Oh, but the darker hours were summoned too.

Try as I might I could not keep from having to admit that had Fern and I by some miracle of cancelled time met in the flesh, she would repudiate me — find out that my Hart blood prevailed over my Worcester — and shamble not unkindly away in the grand manner.

"Oh you would have loved our Fern," my mother used to say to me when I was still young enough to crawl up on her lap. "We all did — so much."

She would tell me how Fern would let little Edna ride on her back — my Aunt Edna whom I always heard of in halting speech and whom I early learned I could never meet though she was not dead. "Perhaps," Mother would say, "— you are no bigger now than Edna was then — perhaps if only Fern were alive today — she would let you ride on her back too. My dear little Ernest you would feel like a little prince. Doesn't that sound like fun?"

Is "fun" the word to describe it? No, "fun" is a word that must be used in a carefree context in which there is no thought of "perhaps." My poor mother, who meant no ill, delicate Margaret in her castle even then dreamt not how much meaning I breathed in along with the perfumes of her warm and innocent body in that simple, "perhaps."

"Oh she was a dandy of a dog," I recall my Dad saying "— almost like a person, Ernie, no kidding. She really liked me, too, you know. Did I ever tell you how she used to bring me the paper before anyone else? It's a damned shame she had to go and get herself killed by that trolley. You know, Peg, we ought to see if we couldn't get Ernie a dog like that."

Oh generous man: his very effusions of love were sacrilege. How I honour the man and how happy I am he died innocent of the meaning of almost everything he uttered. I must — I blush to say this — but I must remind myself of how he will be judged before the throne of God and not according to some lesser standard. My problem, quite clearly, is that I am not so innocent as he. Yet I honour him as one whose worth is established — forever, while mine is still very much in doubt.

The years I think have brought me at times to the calmer waters of objective speculation. I am not now the seventh-grade boy who because of his own consuming faith held his audience, teacher and pupil alike, in the palm of his hand like the top-hatted, golden-tongued orator at a Fourth of July picnic on the town common. Today what I have to say would win the hearts of few schoolchildren, nor would it inspire, because it taps no common faith of any collection of people. I could possibly manufacture a duplicate version of my triumph before Miss Tarnish, but it would be heeded and applauded only by the likes of Annie Ames, Carlton Nixon and a few others left in our little town. The world wobbles on, I tell you, and along with the passing of the old folks comes the creeping doubt that what they had to say and the way they said it had any redeeming value at all. But with all this I can allow no debunking or demythologizing of Fern, for that to happen the child would then not be father to the man. Let me say instead what I perceive, though the perception frequently makes me feel uncomfortably like a traitor.

I see with a kind of visionary clarity a picture of what might have been. I do not feel there is anything wrong in this, for surely the tales of Fern in the Worcester household partook of a rich fictionality—as any fool can see. May I not construct my fiction that Fern, rather than a Worcester dog, had been instead reared among the Harts, my father's people? What then?

There I see her, sprawled under at least two tables at the ice-cream parlours, a town character still, but in a wholly different way, banging her huge tail in indiscriminate greeting to one and all as they entered to partake of the gaudily rich college ices my Grandfather Hart used to prepare for the trade. Oh Fern, would you not naughtily lick the rich cream and cloying syrups from unfinished bowls, be a scandal to the business and be forgiven and grow untidily fat, and be loved by all—receive as lover some ranging mutt of the streets, escaped say from the brutal lash of Denny Poole for a night on the town and fill the crowded rooms behind the curtain in back of the shop with your bounding and rolling puppies? Oh Fern, among the Harts you would have been more human!

Forgive me, Mother Margaret Worcester for this vision, but I know some things I was never told. For one thing I know that Fern had it in her to be Hart as well as Worcester. I know from oblique references and my own deductions what happened between Fern and old Mrs. Halliday—how Fern,unlike anyone else, loved that evil-smelling, mean little old woman and used to kiss her uncontrollably until the old hag threatened lawsuit. And then how it finally happened on an icy winter day—Fern a bounding ton of affection, bestowing love where it couldn't have been less appreciated, flattened the old lady and broke her store-bought spectacles, her right hip and two ribs, and she sued Tom Worcester for as much as he was worth. It is true as well, is it not, that the Halliday lawsuit punctured the balloon of Worcester prosperity even as Edna punctured the one about Worcester respectability, and Fern with unwitting and indiscreet behaviour played a central role in both disgraceful occurrences? Why is it Mother was never told these things? Was it because my name is Hart that no-one could bear to confide in me?

Is it because I am yet a Worcester too that I deny the truth and clothe it under vision or fiction? Do you note that wherever the truth may lie, whoever are villains or saints or human beings merely, however the views may shift, that the figure of Fern is God-like still, altering only according to the mode of the worshipper? You see, Mother, though you would cringe at much of what I am saying, I am loyal yet.

What then does my vision tell me of those other unmentionables—the details of Fern's fatal accident in the path of the trolley on Pine Street and the sudden termination of Edna's claim to an acknowledged place at the Worcesters' hearthside? Is it an imp of Satan, Hart skepticism surfacing at last above the froth of bluff good nature, or merely the fortunate conjunction of the two dire events hitherto decorously kept separated in tales for young ears, but joined at last in the innocent poetic mind of the present mourner—rendering so clear and obvious a sight of death, shame and horror? No matter, the setting, character and defining events merge to focused clarity as intuitive truth, even as three decades of hints and mysterious allusions lock together into logical corroboration.

One must picture Pine Street: the double line of trolley tracks running down the centre of that ample thoroughfare, the shaded walks on either side, the rectory of St. Bridget's church sprawling and somewhat shabby, across the street at some distance from the margin of the public park, which ran in the other direction ultimately up against the back edge of the Worcester property.

On the fateful day, Fern (every movement, even her frolicking ones, had always seemed purposeful and dignified) emerged at an easy trotting pace from the park onto the sidewalk of Pine Street, and peering to the other side over toward St. Bridget's, suddenly yielded to violent and uncharacteristic passion. Heedless of the peril of a rocketing trolley on a mid-morning intown run from the fairgrounds, she sped with fury across the thoroughfare toward two figures she spied over there in lingering conversation — our own Edna and Father Flynn.

What Fern's emotions and thoughts were before she was sideswiped into scrambled and gasping death throes by the gleaming maroon and gold electric car, which itself became derailed and rained down continuing showers of blue sparks onto the gathering crowd, cannot be known; but unfortunately, I deem it now, they could be guessed. See lovely and blooming young Edna kneeling in the gutter of Pine Street with Fern's huge head in her lap and Flynn standing as protectively as he decently could behind her on the sidewalk. Edna sobs uncontrollably while the haze and stink of befouled overhead wires sets the hellish scene, Flynn probably wishing to help, but unable on any terms to intrude.

"Oh Fern," Edna cries, stroking the massive convulsing head of the mythic heart of my dreams, "Oh Fern, can you forgive me? Fern, dearest, I meant no harm."

This spectacle, complete with implied confession, was witnessed by a buzzing crowd, all the members of which in subsequent years, did conspire, more or less, not to feature the embarrassment of poor Edna and Flynn, in the public retelling of Fern legends — at least in my hearing. For what chance would the forgettable ardours of young improper love, soon hustled out of town and out of mind forever, have of being preserved in legend, when compared to the swaggering anecdotal force of canonical Fern stories? Petty domestic anguish has no status in legend, even in the legends of so small a world as the one that I recall. Heroics are what the remembering mind craves; and heroics are what Annie Ames, Carlton Nixon and the rest of that diminishing generation wanted, and got, and will keep for so long as they live.

But since all this is more to me — I have been, as I have tried to show, inheritor, purveyor and victim of the legend — I must complete the vision of the death scene. While Edna cradled the suffering head in her lap, her summer frock bedaubed with slobber and pure-hearted benevolent red blood — that which would not course in my lifetime — she kept crying to the great creature to forgive her, when at last — is it any wonder that I dreamed that I too could be spurned — Fern jerked about (it was her last earthly act) and sank her teeth into the vulnerable, cradling young flesh of Edna's thigh. Fern's last gesture while still mortal — and did not all her actions have deep and obvious meanings? — was to bite poor Edna, who had cried out for her love and forgiveness.

It is, of course, possible to regard Fern's last deed as merely a galvanic and desperate snapping brought on by excruciating pain and no more. But who among those present and especially among those most intimately involved — and I think here of myself not least of all — would be prepared to judge any such action as neutral or devoid of meaning. After all, the Pope himself would have had no less dim a view of what had been going on than Fern herself! And was it not under his authority ultimately that poor Flynn must have been defrocked?

Thus it was that by the time I came into this sad world, Edna was no longer a Worcester and was to us in fact no longer anything but the vague rumour of a lopped branch of the family transplanted, and maybe even flourishing in the faraway sunshine of California. Perhaps, though we don't know how honourable the fellow turned out to be, Edna became a Flynn. I can picture the two of them, no doubt still guiltily twinned; their dreams troubled by the shadowy spirits of both Fern and the Pope, their children — ah, but what of their children? If great shaggy Fern lumbered equivocally through the recesses of my childish imagination, what must she have been, if Edna had been so foolish as to tell them of her, to the little Flynns, provided there were any? Fern could indulge and tolerate Ernest Hart, but Flynns? I hope my cousins were spared any knowledge of the great roaring Fern. But even if they were, the Worcester blood must surely have told in some unimaginable and turbulent way by now. I never fail to read of the strange sects and frenetic lunacies that are characteristic of that state without thinking of what those unloosened and detached cousins of mine there must be up to.

I think, however, that now, even after all the other Harts and Worcesters have gone to their rewards, I should like to take advantage of my lonely state and furnish myself with renewed familial links — perhaps to make up in some way to my Aunt Edna, if indeed she still lives, by spanning the continent in a gesture which no other member of the family has ever seen fit to make.

"I am Margaret's boy," I will say if I can find her, and see what happens then.

"No-one else remembers," I will add, if the prospect seems bright, "only Carlton Nixon and one or two others — they hardly count, do they? There's only little Annie Ames, and she can be forgiven, for after all she owes the fact that she draws the breath of this world to Fern. But there's no-one else."

"Well, yes, there are dozens who have heard the stories, that's true, but they don't remember, and people who can't remember don't believe stories anyway."

What Is Interred with Their Bones

I. Introductory

Those of you who might be interested in the circumstances of Aunt Anna Bolt's death are of several types. It may help to enumerate some of them.

1. Responsible officialdom, in this case a petty officialdom, to be sure, but one which, nonetheless, has its duties to perform. No moral distinctions between nosiness and the ladies' privacy are here an issue. The nursing-home authorities, insurance claims adjustors, estate lawyers, the coroner, keepers of public record—all these in their own prescribed ways must at least process the facts on paper and guard against the uncontrollable flowerings of future complication. I suspect that the unusual nature of the case will, despite the ease with which matters have been dispatched, cause some of them to inquire after the personal motives and feelings involved. I am assuming that some of these functionaries have a human side to them.

2. Relatives, all of us distant ones, but touched all the more by her curious demise in the mere absence of nearer kin. When I say touched, I think I imply motives both admirable and less so. There are the natural unspoken queries as to the disposal of her estate—wondering about its extent and dispersal, but there is also, one hopes, some familial twinge felt through the multifold whole when a close adjunct of the central trunk is lopped away—however sapless and rotted it might be. There are among many of us, I believe, motives hovering somewhere between outright curiosity and love which runs through rivulets of blood easier than through water. Since there are in these times no family chroniclers, each of us yearns to some degree for an intimation of completion, at least, to a part of a story in which we figure, however remotely. Many of us may say,

with a right to the feeling — be it present or no, conscious or subliminal, "Poor Anna Bolt," and mean, thereby, some portion of ourselves.

3. I, the writer of the present account, which is intended to supply the place of family chronicle — to flesh out with human shape and proportion the mainly statistical accounts of officialdom and to supply facts for those whose scattered familial feelings may require some skeleton of empirically verified event. I, in investigating my own motives, cannot claim purity of any kind, though I do think I desire it. Thus it is I take this opportunity to renounce any claim to inheritance, with the exception of the so-called "cottage" at Nit's Cove, which by its total neglect by everyone save me in the last 25 years, I have some uncomplicated claim upon. But for my role as writer: by the workings of a kind of parallax of fate I am tapped for the chore, for I am both distant relative — no matter how connected — and was near at hand by the accident of proximity to the events when they transpired. Upon me, because of the family connection, fell the responsibility of all those duties which are designated in our society to next of kin. Moreover, and here my motives are least pure — I have a mind which has more or less consorted with stories and tales, so that when I think and write of the dear lives of both ladies, Anna and Annie Bolt, I may well be doing no more than plumping them into decorous artistic shapes even as they themselves might perform upon the shapeless slept-upon pillows at the head of their beds of a morning. And, finally,

4. You, the casual reader into whose hands this account may perchance fall. As you read on, in an affair which concerns you not in the least, you may ascribe your motives to nothing very lovely. The lives and deaths of those unrelated to us are usually as dull or as void of significance as last winter's snow, now watery and colloidal only with flotsam, sluicing its way from the gutters of the common streets to the sea. The attendants at the nursing home who had the task of caring for the dead, enfolded, old

ladies' bony bodies when they found them on the bathroom floor, one atop the other, have a need to know how they fell that way in the vice of death—had to know as well, which was Anna, which Annie. So too the kin, for it matters to them whether the final paroxysms were the throes of love or enmity—or, merely the result of their twinned fates; suffering together, as it may have happened, from the chancy, galvanic finger of death. But what might you hope to gain from regarding such a sight? There is no such gore in this account as you may hope to find when hastening toward an auto wreck with a chance to view temples of the human soul lacerated by cruel angular thrusts of jagged steel and glass. These ladies were no werewolves or demons. Their many sins were venial in the extreme, and what they offered upon the great body of goodness in the vastness of time amounted to no more than a negligible and surely unperceived rash of microscopic pinpricks.

There they lay, together on the floor of the bathroom linking their adjacent bedrooms in the Westview Nursing Home, their tiny passions spent, hair down, berobed in the flannel nighclothes of the aged. If you would have truck with such stuff, read on. It would be more wholesome for you to say and feel what I first thought to be the only way for even me to perceive such matters. After all, unusual behaviour on the part of two ladies in their late eighties ought to be attributed to senility and left at that. Is that not what decency would require?

II. Annie & Anna

First of all some matters of fact that are difficult to keep in mind—at least they have so proved to be, even within the family. Anna Bolt, who died one hour after the conclusion of her 88th birthday party, according to her the first that was ever celebrated by a party in her long life, was not a Bolt by birth, but the bride-widow of Annie's brother, Colonel Walker Bolt. So far as anyone remembers, Anna, once Anna Purvis, had no family, no history, no life of any consequence before she was brought blushing and diffident into the Bolt parlour to meet the assembled family in the Christmas season of 1898. Annie Bolt, the affectionate diminutive fixed at that time to make distinction between herself and the gorgeous if unpedigreed addition to the Bolt hearthside, remained a spinster all her life—a true Bolt, in truth only a shade more virginal in her utter purity than her sister-in-law with whom, as chance—or perhaps Colonel Walker Bolt's unconscious choice—would have it, she shared both Christian and family cognomina. Thus, from the time when, a month after his impetuous marriage, the Colonel lost his life in a foreign skirmish—gloriously or not has never been known—these two Bolts, in girlish youth, maturing bloom, aging and aged, and in their death, cleaved to one another. Near of an age, bearing the same name and to all purposes the same fate, is it any wonder that their friends, such as they have, and the more and more remote relatives, found the distinction between them confusing?

To strangers, and possibly to themselves, they seemed closer than sisters, for what parents would have celebrated the arrival of even little twin girls by naming them identically? Why, as years passed and they exchanged memories of what to them was most dear, their love of the dashing young colonel, would not the images of tumbling, happy sibling love—oh, being caught in the strong arms of big brother Walker as one rolled and slid down the precipitous slope of piled hay—and images of courtship and brief connubial happiness—what joy to feel the pain of his bright buttons pressing against one's throbbing bosom—merge, as if in a single consciousness? How could, in 60 or more years, longevity of intimacy and depth of intimacy be kept significantly separated by the mere designation of Mrs and Miss? For all to remember; then, in case it should prove to be of any importance: Annie, the sister—Miss Annie, the true Bolt; Anna, the bride, Mrs. Anna—Mrs. Anna, the chosen love of the beloved Colonel Walker. Need it also be noted that he, coming to the age for selecting a mate, should have chosen one whose beauty and bearing resembled almost uncannily her whom he had heretofore taken as his measure of female excellence, his dear sister, Annie?

At the time of their deaths, Anna and Annie were, among the occupants of the Westview Nursing Home, the longest residents; that, coupled with their somewhat regal bearing, gave them minor privileges and a certain natural deference from all. This, it seems easy to understand, was shared by them equally, and with a punctiliousness that made observance a shade difficult for everyone else. Thus it was that when old Ellen Pritzker died, her chum, Miss Schulz, was moved to a downstairs room and the Bolts were given two handsome front rooms, each with a view of the river, and the fateful bathroom between. Which of the ladies was to inherit the former quarters of Miss Schulz, clearly a maid-in-waiting for the queenly old Pritzker? Her room, it came to be realized, held no perceptible inferiority other than its former association with a lesser figure, and the matter was decided girlishly by the Bolts themselves, on the flip of a coin — tails for Mrs. Anna, Miss Schulz's old room — ever after not a jot less desirable nor imposing for visitors than the former quarters of the deceased Pritzker next door.

"Come in," either of them was wont to say upon receiving visitors, "and sit down. I'll run next door and get Anna/ie." The other residents fell into the pattern of knocking on their doors alternately upon successive visits, each seeming a mirror image of the last.

III. The Birthday Party

The following account of the birthday party, Anna's 88th birthday but her first party ever, as she cooed excitedly to her guests many times during the evening, and of the events following, has been reconstructed from the testimony of the guests, of Rudy Varnum, who was putting away chairs while Anna and Annie lingered, and of Miss Walsh, who observed Anna's hysterical ascent to the second floor on the chair elevator, the events thereafter with facts pieced together from information divulged by members of the home staff.

The party itself: gala, warm and a shade on the sentimental side, Anna's eyes filling with tears several times, though she smiled through them — radiantly, as Mrs. Van der Holz described it afterward. Everyone was affected by Anna's revelation that in all her 88 years, there had never been a special party just for her.

"Imagine that," Mrs. Van der Holz said.

"So you see," Anna continued, "this makes you all very dear to me in a very special way."

After the first rubber of whist, three tables in all, the double doors of the parlour opened, and Rudy Varnum dressed in a chef's outfit wheeled in a tea-table with an immense tiered birthday cake on it. The applause and gasps were loud and sincere. It must have had all 88 candles on it, every one ablaze — a veritable soaring fairy castle of lights and delicate scrolled frosting. Rudy beamed and bowed.

"I — I don't know what to say," Anna breathed. "I've — I've never had a birthday cake before!"

The servings Anna dispensed from the lower tier were generous, and second helpings were offered and accepted. Hearty quantities of coffee and tea were consumed, yet the urns were still plenteously filled and the edifice of the great cake was barely scarred.

"We'll let everyone have a piece at lunch tomorrow, if it's all right with you, Miss Anna," Rudy said, smiling and bowing.

Anna, eyes misty, asked the room at large if they, dear friends as they all were, could imagine how she and Annie looked when they were just girls — would they like to see?

"I do feel girlish tonight," she said. And then pausing, eyes ashine, to look over at the great cake: "after all, why shouldn't I?"

Before the excited outburst of approval had subsided, Annie left the parlour to fetch the large family album from their rooms upstairs.

"Oh, you must have been lovely young belles," Mrs. Van der Holz crowed, a sentiment which produced murmured seconds from all.

"Oh, they're still heartbreakers now, ain't they?" Rudy winked, and everyone giggled, as they often did at Rudy's bold joshing.

"Rudy, you're scandalous," Anna said, feigning sharpness. "But I can hardly be cross with anyone at the very first birthday party I've ever had."

"There now," Anna said, the album open to a page containing but a single picture, a browned photograph of two young belles indeed. In billowy gowns they simpered at the photographer with heads turned toward him, though they faced the left-hand frame. "Which one is me and which one is dear Annie? Can you tell?"

"Why they're both lovely," said Mrs. Van der Holz.

"What a frisky caper," said Miss Schulz, alluding to the graceful dance step they appeared to be executing in unison, the girl behind clasping the one in front around the waist, and the two of them together kicking their left legs aloft, the tops of their high shoes revealed for all to see.

"What merry little devils you must have been," someone said. "I must say I couldn't tell which is which!"

"So fresh and saucy-looking," said another.

"Two charming lassies," Mrs. Van der Holz sighed, "so alike and yet really beauty of two quite different types."

"How do you mean?" Miss Annie asked.

"Why look here," Miss Schulz cried out, pointing to the left arm of the girl behind, "she's got her hand clenched into a fist! Why you'd almost think she was going to sock her one!"

Mrs. Van der Holz began to giggle. "Why you're right, Effie, see how her arm is crooked—as if she were going to give her a—a haymaker, do they call it?"

Anna's finger ran over the old photograph as she blinked in the expressionless way that old ladies sometimes do, and then she said, breaking into a smile, "Well, I must say."

She reached over to grasp Annie's wrinkled hand and announced as if it were the greatest joke in the world, "My dear friends, you may guess all night, but it won't do you a bit of good. Annie and I ourselves can no longer recall which is which."

Miss Annie placed her other hand over Anna's. "We're both very old ladies now, aren't we dear?"

The sadder tone alerted Rudy, who was still clearing away. "But still with lots of pepper," he said. "Still with lots of pepper."

IV. Rudy Varnum & Mrs. Walsh

It was Rudy who was sole witness to what happened in the parlour after the guests had left. He described it in the following way, as best I can recall. Here, I'd rather give only what I know from my one witness.

"Well, Mr. Short, for a long time they just set there talking so low I couldn't hear what they was saying—not that I was tryin to hear anyway. You know, I'd have a lot to do to listen to everything these old gals here say, half of them not quite right—and these two as well, or one of them anyway, though I never would have guessed it before. They always seemed plenty full of starch to me, and awful sharp.

"Anyway, they stood up and started to leave the parlour holding hands together. You know, like it was a sentimental occasion, which it was of course—88 years and never had a birthday party, think of that! Well, they stopped by the cake, and I know what I heard from here on because it was so queer and unexpected. I've gone over it in my mind several times afterward—what with them both passing on that same night.

"Miss Annie said something like this, 'It's a beautiful cake, Anna dear, just a beautiful cake, what a lovely memory.' And then: 'But didn't you think the frosting smelt very strange?' Well, this perked me up to notice, because I certainly didn't think there was anything wrong with the frosting, not at all, but it was a trick, you see, and Mrs. Anna fell for it—well, who wouldn't? Who would have thought it?

"I saw all this and no mistake. As soon as Mrs. Anna bent over to smell, Miss Annie gave the back of her head a smart little push, just enough to mush her face right in the cake but good. Before Mrs. Anna knew what happened Miss Annie had hopped right out of that parlour and probably went up the back stairs to her room. I don't know about that part of it.

"I come right over to Mrs. Anna to see what I could do, but she wouldn't take no help from me. She just began to bawl and howl in the worst way you ever heard. I don't know how she could even see where she was headed, with all that frosting under her glasses and everywhere, but she made the front hall and climbed onto the chair elevator and up she went howling like a wild Indian all the way. After that, I never saw her till after she was dead."

Miss Walsh, who occupied the desk in the downstairs hall that night, saw Mrs. Anna emerge from the parlour and make her way to the chair elevator and then ride up, howling just as Rudy Varnum had said. She, too, tried to help and calm her down, but Mrs. Anna would not be comforted or divulge any information. "Well, Mr. Short, it took me by surprise, as you can guess. At first I didn't recognize who it was, all that strange white substance all over her face. I just couldn't guess what had happened. I honestly first recognized her by her dress.

"No, she didn't say anything I could recognize as words, just a horrible crying and moaning. Do you know, when I ran up the stairs beside her I noticed five or six candles sticking out at all different angles from her face. It was awful; they were like crazy blue whiskers a child might stick onto a snowman."

V. In the Bathroom

After Miss Annie fled, presumably up the back stairs to her room and Mrs. Anna made her roaring ascent up the chair elevator to hers, there were no witnesses to the events that followed — all is inference, a process which, considering the officially morbid scrutiny applied to the remains and my own not unskilled probing as a questioner, is certainly superior to mere guesswork. Of course they died of heart failure, a matter easily established. Their hearts had, in death, stopped beating, and it is a fair supposition that being distraught — both bodies so delicate and vulnerable — they gave up their twinned lives as a consequence of some mutual emotional tumult. May we name such a death-dealing process by what is merely dismissive in other contexts? Bickering? A spat? Scrapping or fighting?

Whatever we may call it, the authorities — Miss Walsh, who was first to say, "Don't you think we had better risk an intrusion and go in anyway," and Mrs. Dunn who replied, "Very well, I shall assume the responsibility if you will countersign the report," found them slumped together there in the bathroom, which like so many other things, they shared. Both of them had divested themselves of their party finery and had prepared for retiring — for their doom as it turned out — by donning their flannel nightclothes. Mrs. Dunn, new as a night superior, expressed her confusion, like that of so many others, saying as she bent over to confirm her suspicions as to their state, "Here's a pretty fix, Walsh, they're both dead. Can you help me tell which is which?" Miss Walsh, trailing behind Mrs. Dunn as befitted a subordinate, had not yet entered the bathroom (for one thing there was not enough room for four of them). From Miss Annie's bedroom she peeped over Mrs. Dunn's shoulder and replied, "That's easy, Mrs. Dunn, Mrs. Anna is the one with the cake-frosting on her face."

Indeed, she was correct. Whatever preparations Anna had made for going to bed, she, for some reason, had not included among these removing the sticky white confection with any degree of efficiency. True, an examination of Anna's room revealed, turning up a crumpled tissue near her dresser, that she had taken one swipe at it and had perhaps plucked out the embedded candles, but that was all. In the rigidity of death her contorted features, partly masked, partly made more hideous by the still clinging gobs of sweet, decorative topping, gave, as Mrs. Dunn—she who was no stranger to death-scenes—put it, "a spooky effect." Miss Annie, admittedly more lovely in her repose, bore no marks of struggle or perturbation save one: the front of her nightgown was drenched with water, still icy to the touch when Mrs. Dunn felt of it soon after entering the bathroom.

Not all the expertise of Mrs. Dunn and later of the doctor could perform the miraculous and revive either of the two, though no-one could be faulted in the efforts of their ministrations. Miss Walsh noted and gave up the information to any who would ask, and some few did, that Mrs. Anna had fallen atop Miss Annie and not the other way about.

VI. What Must Have Happened

In a case such as the present one the investigator who tries to reconstruct events and explain motives is obliged to take into account the improbable—for the events that were witnessed and attested to were certainly bizarre enough to set off a chain of subsequent grotesqueries. Once admitting the unlikely event of Annie's small, slight-handed push—such a childish little trick, possibly so fleeting a motivation—the consequences would be liable to burgeon in all their wild abnormality. The implausible, happening once and established as fact, prepares us to admit aberration as the expected, at least until the string—whatever that may signify—runs out. Put another way, one eccentricity implies the presence of more jinks that are likely (back now to the plausible, you see) to produce such physiological results as dumped adrenalin, racing pulse and subsequently collapse and then demise.

Thus, reconstruction commences, and the first, most easily accountable event, is the dousing of Annie by a vindictive Anna. The stainless-steel pitcher together with some dozen and a half remnants of ice-cubes discernible on the bathroom floor when Miss Walsh entered, seem to point to that explanation.

The drenched flannel robe supports the theory rather well. I felt at first that the presence of a pitcher of ice-water in one of the ladies' rooms might have led me to a clue: a special request having been made by one of them at some time during the course of the evening, but, alas, all I could learn was that Mrs. Anna required ice-water on her nightstand every night before retiring, her penchant for gulping it nightly at such an hour being a long-standing eccentricity and a marvel much discussed among staff members. So, the pitcher is linked to Anna easily enough.

What appears to have happened is that Anna, after sobbing in her room for a few minutes (Mrs. Walsh was kindly listening outside, having been repulsed in her efforts to help and comfort), undressed, and in so doing, peered at her grotesque face in the mirror. After a daub at the frosting with a tissue, she became heated with the thought of vengeance and picked up the icy pitcher from her night-stand and stalked to the bathroom. From her final position on the floor and from other evidence, we know that Miss Annie had been seated on the toilet. It is likely that in such a posture she received the massive shock of a pitcher full of ice-water squarely upon her thin chest. Mrs. Walsh testifies that about the time that this assault must have taken place, she did hear, not a scream, but more of a "yip" sound, like the single bark of a nervous little puppy. It was not long after that she and Mrs. Dunn decided upon forcing entry.

The simplest explanation, then, of Annie's death is that she was murdered, the weapon being a pitcher of ice-water. That there was no bruise upon her body suggests that Anna did not heave pitcher and all at her, but the contents only, a fact which, if the matter had come to charges, might have reduced the action to manslaughter. But of course no such matter need be settled or even considered, for almost immediately Mrs. Anna must have toppled onto the prone form of her sister-in-law and herself expired, the accumulated passions of the evening culminating at this point. Whether her mortal thread was severed as her consciousness registered the lethal consequences of her deed cannot be known. One hopes, if she had come to this realization, that among the shocks she had received during the eventful evening, not least, and perhaps even crucial, was remorse for her own folly. We human beings cannot resist the appeal of such symmetries, whether our hunger be for the aesthetic or for moral justice the icy cascade of water on poor mortal flesh all unprepared, as against a similar cold dousing of the conscience by the shocking knowledge of one's utter responsibility.

VII. The Clue in the Kleenex Box

The true shape of history is to be comprehended best as running from the thickness of experienced, present event, which may be grasped with assurance and mental tranquillity and officially recorded, through ever thinning gradations of deduction, inference, guesswork, until as was said before, the string runs out. Here is the place where one finds the mere airy junk that one collects for love or to feed some other dementia. Here the spider-thin threads tying us to what has become the past may be the rediscovered continuation of that run-out string, now visible, now invisible, or they may be merely ropy effluvia dangling from walls and roof in the cave of ignorance. Who can say? As for myself in the present case, I encountered at a later date an artifact which is compelling enough to anyone who may yet care, though damnably inconclusive still. Such residue as the following may be regarded, if you will, as visible knots in the now-invisible thread.

The events of life may well be explained by natural laws, but they are quirky nonetheless. At the time of the deaths of Anna and Annie Bolt and the subsequent investigation I was cursed with a heavy, annoying, dripping, head cold, and as a consequence carried with me, on even the briefest foray outside my house, a long, but flat box of Kleenex, which fitted neatly inside my attache case. However it happened, I must at some time during the few afternoons I spent in the Bolts' rooms at Westview have exchanged my own box for one that was lying about in one of the two rooms — I curse my stars that I cannot, for all my powers of reconstruction, remember which one — I was in both extensively, and in both laid out my papers and answered pertinent correspondence concerning the affair. I must merely confess my carelessness and plead remorse to all — if indeed there are any really — who have some stake in this business. It was only some time afterward that I found in a box of Kleenex, in my own house, no less — another cold causing me to search my supplies for tissues to carry with me once more — a message on a single sheet of folded paper tucked under what must have been the top few layers of Kleenex. The find, inconclusive as it was, nonetheless had an archaeological feel to it: here under several strata of tissue, hastily placed no doubt, was something tangible. Could this be the very box from which Mrs. Anna had plucked the one tissue she used that fateful evening in a futile, hasty attempt to clear her visage of the loathed frosting? No, that would be to assume what in no way is warranted, even as a supposition.

The message itself, alas, was devilish in seeming to explain and clarify, but really doing no more than providing further speculative variables, and, incidentally, implicating needlessly a third figure, whose part in the whole affair I am convinced to have been benignly innocent.

The note was printed in large, shaky block letters — yes, I have already considered the possibility of identifying the hand, and it is impossible to do. It read simply as follows: "DEAR RUDY, DARE NOT CHOOSE BETWEEN US. LOVE, ANN."

You can well imagine how petty-spirited I felt when I could not resist the temptation to confront poor Rudy with this note. I squirmed at my own effrontery, but pressed on, driving through the traffic to Westview like a man possessed by demons. Surely if Rudy had done something to bring on this scrawled but undelivered piece of petulance, he would dismiss it now as unimportant. It was unthinkable that he had in any conscious way held out to either Anna or Annie the tormenting prospect of passionate love; he was a universally beloved 70-year-old handyman, whose joshing courtliness, everyone thought at least, merely brightened the day of all the ladies at Westview. He was indistinguishable from the other male residents except that he received a small salary and performed duties, such as those which brought him to the scene on the fateful night. True, he sometimes cruised the corridors of the ladies' wing, with no more excuse than delivering the mail from downstairs (an unnecessary task), and was forever cracking jokes about his harem and how jealous the old fellows were of his privileges, but if ever man distributed even such as these small favours and attentions upon womankind more impartially, it was not because Rudy lacked in fairmindedness, or universal and undiscriminating cheer. Showing him the note would merely introduce to his serene mind the possibility that he in some way, through an unremembered and unintended slight, would have to share in the responsibility for what had happened.

I needn't have worried about this, as it turned out, for after I had arrived at Westview and closeted myself with Rudy and showed him the note, he shook his head and chuckled, "Well now, don't that beat the cars. It's funny how they can get crazy, and we don't even know it, till one day it shows up."

I simply couldn't bring myself to intercept his cheery acceptance of general senile lunacy with any thing so crass as asking, "Which one, Rudy?" To him it clearly would have made no difference. From his perspective his entire harem, as it were, were on the same treadmill toward mental disintegration and final oblivion. The last thing he said to me before I left, apologizing and intarticulate, stinging myself with the question, "What had I come for?" was the comment, "You know, Mr. Short, I always miss them when they go, but them two especially. They was always so full of pepper. Yes sir, they was always plenty full of pepper."

VIII. The Family Album

The questions that officialdom need not ask but which kinfolk can presumably care about are sometimes answered by pawing through the memorabilia that the laity keep of themselves, for themselves and for their own issue. Less official than the now largely defunct family Bible with its quasi-legal entries and the presumed divine sanctioning of their properly recorded individual existences, is the family album, which in the heyday of Anna and Annie consisted mainly of photographs — now already mottled and embrowned. There I turned in those confused days after the two deaths, finding the huge, scuffed, velvet-covered tome among the worldly effects of Anna Bolt. Miss Walsh informed me on the night of the party it had been left in the parlour with the gifts and had then been returned to Anna's room because it was there that the presents should obviously be placed. It seemed fitting enough that the gifts that Anna had received should be given back to their donors as tokens of remembrance of her whom her friends had gathered to honour, and so they were; but the album was the property of Annie as well as Anna, and, with only a few compunctions, I felt that it was now mine to keep. I fancied that it might contain insight into matters that only a relative need care about, and of all the relatives only I seem to have even semi-official family uses to which it can be put. I intend to be punctilious about the matter of the cottage property at Nit's Cove, and, indeed, anticipate legal imbroglios in order for me to sustain my just claim to it. Think of the discriminations we make: the box of Kleenex was so trifling an item that I unconsciously walked off with it, though it contained a most private, if fizzling, little bomb; the album I consciously appropriated, though doing so cost me some twinges of guilt; the cottage property — the least interesting because it had been untouched by Anna and Annie for 25 years — I will receive only after other claims have been legally made and publicly spurned by a court of law. Thus it is we read the value of our poor passions and private lives.

The album, then, which I carried somewhat lovingly to my quarters in order to peruse it at my own hearthside, revealed, I'm afraid, a hint of what Rudy perceived in assuming with his worldly chuckle that distinctions between Anna and Annie are in the last analysis of negligible importance — an inevitable truth, I suppose, but one which I have been resisting and still resist in the face of all. I seem to have a kind of loyalty, but loyalty to whom or what I cannot determine; for Anna and Annie, the very keepers of the album, had been so negligent as to label pictures only sporadically, and when they did, very imperfectly, as I discovered from finding a portrait of myself as an infant labelled "Lawrence?" there being to my knowledge no-one in the family of that name.

Most of my leafing through the old album put me in an extremely dispirited mood, as I found I was capable of identifying almost none of the characters there enshrined—aunts, uncles, cousins, inlaws and so on, to say nothing of the innumerable neighbours and friends—not that I could even assign persons to their proper categories. I found I was not very sure, indeed rather unsure, of the identity of my own parents in their salad days—a time which I have always enjoyed picturing in my mind's eye.

What I found to my surprise, however, is that I could invariably recognize Anna and Annie—that is, they were unmistakable as one or the other of the two aunts. In my mind, then, they had achieved, in tandem, an historical existence more sharply focused than that of any other members of my family. I was, I discovered, utterly confident that I could identify without the slightest chance of mistake, the two relatives which I could with sure predictability never distinguish.

One wonders how these facts bear one upon the other. May we say that individual identity was enhanced by its being doubled; the loss being only on the order of two, whereas the rest of the family was each lost into the vague morass to be named generally as "Bolt-relative"? Indeed, many pictured there in the album, perhaps not related, perhaps so, can only be dated roughly by the decade, according to their clothing, and be said to have been inhabitants of eastern North America. How much better to live on in the vigour of human memories as a "paired alternative" or as a "binary option."

I was engaged with just such musings as these when, turning a page, my attention was suddenly taken by the old daunting problem once more. Two facing leaves were given over to several small snapshots from different eras, though Annie and Anna were in each. Someone had lettered "Birthdays" rather crudely at the top of the left-hand page. In each snapshot Annie and Anna, in party finery distinguishable by era of fashion, could be seen on either side of, behind, in front of or in some varying spatial relationship with a birthday cake, usually an impressively large and ornate one. Naturally I thought of Anna's repeated claim on the evening of her 88th birthday: that she had never had a party before. If this photographic display of natal anniversaries was a record of Annie's birthdays only, what, then, had angered her on the night of Anna's innocent party at Westview? Or, had Anna been lying, Annie feeling that Anna's innuendoes of neglect had unjustly reflected upon her or upon the Bolts' generosity? The fused image of Anna-Annie that I had formed in my mind but moments before now began to tug apart once again. After all, at least one of these ladies, whether she had wholly intended to or not, had killed the other. Perhaps they were both culpable and like the calico cat and the gingham dog had destroyed one another. Was the image of two-as-one still imaginable? Could two fused human beings commit suicide by killing each other?

Such thoughts are, I know, folly, but they are no less so than my subsequent actions in playing historian-detective once more—on the assumption that investigation could separate what seemed so devilishly joined. I refused to give up the possibility of pairings such as: the guilty and the innocent, the dominant and the submissive, the tyrant and the martyr—and, indeed, the virgin and the wife. What is worse, I'm afraid, I had never wholly abandoned a distinction that I recognized had been operating subliminally all along: the one between Bolt and Purvis, the distinction between blood and water. Ah, what nasty things there are that history wants to know.

This time it seemed inevitable that my researches would end as shamefully as had my grilling of Rudy, and so they proved to do. Yet, I could not help myself. Most of the birthday celebrations captured by the camera had been held outdoors—happy garden-parties, they appeared. Anna's birthday was in mid-June, the date I well knew from my own involvement soon after the dire event. But what of Annie? If her birthday should happen to have fallen in the winter months, the lineaments of a story/tale/explanation would begin to emerge. I called Mrs. Dunn at Westview for the information. I guiltily told her, though it was the truth itself, after a fashion, that I was engaged in writing a family history. The answer, however, was of little help; Annie's birthday was August 30th.

But not wholly daunted, I purchased a reading-glass and attempted, but failed, to determine from the foliage of the trees and the garden flowers in bloom which of the two dates was more likely. With what eye-straining scrutiny did I pore over those photographs, only to be defeated at last. If only I could have discerned from the undistinguishable blobs of foliage and happy blooms of yesteryear the characteristic pyramidical heaps of late blooming lilacs (Anna) or the nodding faces of early asters, those harbingers of cool autumn (Annie), I might have been prompted to lean in one direction or the other—toward the bride, the liar, Anna of June, insatiable in celebrating feasts for herself and believing to the last that they have never happened at all, her Colonel, her bridegroom, long dead and buried away under foreign soil; or toward the eternal vestal, the true Bolt, Annie of ultimate August, for whom repeated festival could never be sufficient recompense for her spinsterish state, even her very brother, her male alter-ego, her Platonic, male polestar obliterated from her firmament.

But as always, the further one examined the more the two merged to a general July blur of green lawn, parasol, happy, frosted cake full-flowering either/or. To repeat the words of Mrs. Van der Holz I could see only "Oh you must have been beautiful young belles." But the more I examined, the more the words of Miss Schulz upon seeing the dancing photograph came back to me. "What a frisk caper!" she had said and then gone on to see, amid the youthful frolicking, the clenched fist, the possibility within the expression of bodily high spirits of the ultimate haymaker.

What could I see from these smaller photographic mementoes of birthday feasts? I turned my attention from foliage and flower, and, perhaps because I was looking for it, found, I think, either Anna or Annie mocking me from the other side of the grave. I have said that the snapshots were all small and detail captured on them is not reliable — but here is what I think I can see: a table upon a green lawn amid flowers and scattered lawnchairs, upon the table a pile of gifts as yet unopened, and in the centre a cake with a single candle, and, bending over it as if to remove the first slice, a beautifully coiffured Anna or Annie. Peeking rakishly around from behind is an equally beautiful Anna or Annie laughing in what seems to be the appropriate high spirits of the occasion. There, above the head of the lovely mature woman cutting the cake may be seen two fingers, spread apart and aloft in the timeless childish gesture representing asses' ears. Or at least they seem more likely to be that than two whitish branches of the tree one can see in the background over Annie/Anna's head. I am not 100% confident, however, though by now I have examined the photograph a thousand times at least.

IX. Epilogue

So it is that officialdom is content to let these two long-lived ladies lapse into the tomb, with no more questions to be asked than appears seemly. The family, if I am its representative, has felt it necessary to ask more, to probe more deeply into what is mysterious, or just bewildering, with regard to Annie and Anna. But it may not be correct for me to assume that I do represent the far-scattered Bolts. Perhaps, they, like Rudy, would be content to love them both firmly and happily, but indiscriminately, though the truth might well be that one had visited torment or niggling and eroding hatred upon the other for several decades. It is possible, however, that my inquiry may merely reveal my own rather sickly fantasies, though I sincerely hope not; I hope what I have done has sprung from a kind of love that is deeper and more abiding—no, more valuable and more frustrating—than Rudy's, though I always would like to honour that good man's name.

But what of you who represent neither officialdom nor caring or uncaring kin? Anna and Annie, seen at the last, had wrapped themselves in a single seed or shell of privacy—so much seems to have been deliberate. For me to pry them apart is in some measure necessary. You have glimpsed their sundering in that repulsive bathroom scene; but having glimpsed that cracking of solidarity, do not forget the union which their entangled bodies represented at the last. Though the union was possibly one of passionate enmity, it was indeed a union. Unless you are willing to grant that the Bolts, for all their eccentricities, their far-flung destinies, are, and should live in memory as, a unit, you come away from this whole narrative as voyeurs, curiosity seekers, who frustratingly find no thrills; for what else in God's world could their poor lives and ridiculous deaths represent?

III. Other Prose

Wobblings and Warblings

Being asked to say something about poetry, I find the impulse to be irresponsible almost completely overpowering. I don't think it is just nervousness, either. Would nervousness make me come up with, "Poems ought to be like the way old snow discolours under the birdhouse?" That bewildering remark may even be a poem beginning itself in answer to a question that seems to call for a statement of conviction. I can construct utterances that sound like convictions easily enough, and then I find I'm not sure I want to be convicted. So it is that there is wobbling between things that sound like something, and something else again. Every now and then those wobblings strike me as warblings—oh, I certainly do hope they sometimes are warblings—human equivalents to birdsong, much of which, they tell me, is functional in nature. Human beings warble such things—full-throated and with wide open beaks—as, "The knives and forks go in the other drawer," and, "Oh, I don't know, it doesn't look so bad to me." The impulse to be irresponsible is perhaps trying to be true to fused wobbling/warbling. Yet no one can be irresponsible without wearing some of the clothing of responsibility. I believe in, and can be convicted of, having my bare feet on underneath my shoes and socks.

Thus, some other convictions:

A. My poems need to coast along on something: celebration, curse, wish, a line of malarkey, worried maunderings, fevered dreams, opportunistic and desperate rostrum-grabbing, mimicry—anything which in the course of common life is likely to uncork the bottle of eloquence—not just accomplished and suave eloquence, but all kinds—especially *failed* eloquence. Failed eloquence is, in my view, often just lovely poetry, provided it is invented poetry pretty much on the spot and not just something formulaic out of the movies or off the TV.

B. All sorts of so-called prose is really poetry, but people feel better if they are allowed to continue to call it prose. This is the Monsieur Jourdain business geared up for modern times.

C. Much poetry has to do with lost causes.

D. Only the censors believe in the real power of words. Protect poets from those who say, "It doesn't make any difference what the kids read; they see those things written on walls anyway." Poets should not choose as allies those who say that words don't matter.

E. Life is full of poetry if you are careful never to come right out and say that life is full of poetry—unless you are pretending to be fooling, or unless you are pretending to be serious.

F. The most interesting poetry for me is that which occupies a space that is waiting for it that didn't seem to be there before. Good art colonizes what we didn't even know needed mapping.

G. Since time began, billions of greetings cards with verses on them have been sent back and forth amongst people. Doubtless very few of them have expressed messages with any degree of precision. Yet how many messages want to be sent! We must be content with displacements of intent and poetry has to accommodate itself—no, not to greeting-card verse, but to the truth these billions of failed/successful messages represent: the human need for displacement. "Happy birthday, you old goat. You're not getting any younger!" See? "A bouquet of roses for Grandma across the miles." It is possible that our culture took a turn for the worse when so-called "studio cards" first made their appearance.

H. Through history much poetry depended on courtship—i.e., saying things you don't mean, exactly, and remaining somewhat confused over long periods of time. Whenever courtship declines in practice—or the conscious belief in it declines—poetry is in for harder times. You can court the muse herself, but that is harder because you have to get drawn into knowing what it is you wanted after it happened.

I. The world is in the dreadful state it is because of people who believe in high seriousness and then turn right around and try to practise it.

Titles for 25 Familiar Essays

Tact
Deathbed Promises
The Gadfly
Counting Things: A Compulsive Pastime
On Threading Mazes
The Ubiquitous Terrapin
So You Think You Know Kale
Water Over the Dam
Are You One of the Linchpins of Society?
The Ovary: Nature's Deepest Mystery
The Forgotten Art of Whistling
The Locust and You
How to Talk About the Weather
Famous Villains of Literature
Whatever Happened to Quotable Poets?
What Kind of Dogfood Did Pavlov Use?
My First Waterspout
Bland Food, A New Adventure in Dining
Dancing With Neither Belt Nor Suspenders
Fear of Voting
Concerning the End of the World
Optimism—Your Best Option in Spite of Statistics
On the Pleasures of Being Mawkish
Brevity
The Five Most Famous Smudges in History

Bauer family portrait, 1980
Left to right, standing: John, William and Ernest
Seated: Grace and Nancy

"Some Kind of Chronicle at Least": A 1984 Journal

Editor's note: *In Bauer's archives sits a purple-covered, hard-bound 1984 Daily Journal, with a lined page for each day of the year, the title printed on the cover by Brownline Inc., the maker of the blank book of 14-inch-tall pages. For the first six weeks of 1984 Bauer was faithful to the journal, usually writing on the assigned day but sometimes falling behind and catching up. A process he adopted was to fill up every line of each large page and to use no paragraph breaks, despite frequent jumping from topic to topic. (None of the journal entries are transcribed here in their entirety. Though I've abridged, while usually keeping whole sentences intact, I decided not to distract the reader with many strings of ellipsis, instead reflecting the original style of unsignalled focus-switches.) The journal entries often cover morning, afternoon and night — not always chronologically — but in their freedom they include digressions, questionings and afterthoughts. A collage-like effect is created by the many layers of Bauer's life: his reading and teaching, his happy interactions with his wife and sons (his daughter was in university in Sackville for most of the six weeks), aesthetics, self-awareness, his varied artistic projects, and the journal-writing itself. After February 15, the rest of the blank book remained blank. Like nothing in Bauer's previously published work, his journal experiment reveals the day-to-day life of a curiosity-driven, imaginatively restless, entertaining, humane, word-nimble man.*

Sunday, January 1

Clear and merely cool (-10°) at most. A few kiwis struggle in the cups, not wholly established as yet. The grapefruit shows little life. It is probably a contest with time — can't last until it is repotted and responds to spring? Nor did some (however) tiny degree of outdoor work transpire. Foiled by late rising, football on TV and waiting for Ernie. He and Angela arrived from Quebec on the train-bus from Moncton two hours late. Everybody is at home.

A roast beef dinner and wonderful conversation. Projects burgeon in the mind. Ernie's new book on Canadian folk art—wooden objects and surfaces. How beautiful and loving is the camera work to display these handmade and often-handled objects. Displayed with superb lighting and subtle-toned background they seem to surpass themselves. What a cover for a book most of these photos would be. The bolted and gaudily painted bird-bath support, angular and irregular (yet holding the cement saucer level). How to select paints and surfaces that would endure the outdoors? Hearing but not cogitating the football score on TV from downstairs. The mind was able to *refer* to the audible rumble and recall the sounds in the abstract and *then* hear anew (to comprehend) the score. Was this all a function of preoccupations and alertness (or readiness) of the mind to put responses to work in multiple directions. Projects, worries, chores and ideas were layered many deep, each to be disposed of in priorities as occasion or pressure or desire demands. This is the pattern of the mind juggling, evading guilt, embarassment, being caught by unpleasant surprise. We need a plumber again so soon for faucets. *Buddenbrooks* makes me remember how good it is in parts. The house, the Christmas, what music means, the treatment of disease (specifics—symptoms—the death already happened). The Baltic seashore on their holidays. Washington rolled over the Rams 57–7. Tomorrow *should be* at least 20 below with the axe outside and a host of 1000 papers done.

Monday, January 2

Marked papers all day to produce feelings of virtue. Did not watch Bowl games until tonight where now the Orange Bowl is on and half way through. 17–17 tie at present. Miami-Nebraska. Thoughts working together. 90% of the adult population is visually illiterate, says George Nelson in *How to See: In A World God Never Made*. The recommendation to use a 6 by 4" viewfinder and to make scribble drawings. Does such a device constitute a legitimate aid in combating this illiteracy or laziness of sight (too sleepy watching the Orange Bowl to its exciting conclusion.)

Back to Nelson and Carl Nickel, *Creating and Painting in Watercolor*. I am interested to make a viewfinder to surreptitiously look at the world to see what I can see. The viewing part I suspect is easy but the scribbling may be something else. I have access to an almost unlimited number of felt tip pens, so perhaps piles of scrap 8½ x11 paper could be made into a junk sketch pad. Can I find time, place, and gall to run around sketching. I would hope so. How many faces are there in your living room? Most people presumably underestimate radically how many facial representations surround them in their normal quarters—any represented faces, people, animals, mythical beings, etc. how many little imagined eyes peering here and there! Also: I recall my obsession with mailboxes and washing on lines on my trips to Newcastle and Bathurst. Would I need special lenses to avoid the trespass of photographing such items from the car—to avoid getting out of the car? I heard on the radio that Pablo Casals as a very young boy knew the piano and organ but had never seen a cello until some travelling musicians came through the town with a home-made one. His father—what a father—constructed one from a large gourd!

Wednesday, January 4

The clear weather continues for yet another day. For yet another day the outdoor work project is put off. I felt rushed to work to spend the entire day in administrative work for writing courses. A rush of not wholly unpleasant blandness, but precluding any mental life, advance of worthy causes, etc. Lunch in the office chawing on a sandwich while students tapped at the door. [It was a] grim movie that Ernie, Grace, Paul, and Angela went to tonight: intrigue and blood and guts. I am getting more and more jealous of what I do and how I spend my thinking, viewing, and doing life. If there is a thirst for the visual world, there is also something of a comparable thirst for the new and productive, or possible fresh ideas. What is the common element in these yearnings. Toward what. Something I can use—which seems to relate to connected action: Color, money, force, growth. Revised:

Construction, security, energy, the organic. How does an interest in one's own mind arrange to interpenetrate with all of these? The faith I guess is that the doing will reveal some of the connections. All of this does partake of the appetitive (hunger, thirst) more than of the cerebral or rational (whatever the word is for taking the world and meanings as fixed, known, as others would have it). My viewfinder, my axe, my brushes, my darkroom all languish. Tools for making strokes and marks on things. Is it enough to leave marks—and, will the marks in any way bespeak the joy of the action? More A. R. Humphreys [*The Augustan World: Life and Letters in Eighteenth-century England*] who *does* give us an age of doers and joyous perceivers. Glitter, vistas (*arenas* for action): is this the adventuring spirit—related to the venturing spirit.

Saturday, January 7
A drizzly day with some notable events. Grace and Paul left on the noon bus and left the house strangely quiet. Ernie and John went to the French Centre to play racquet ball *and* I finally—on the seventh day of this new year—got outdoors—it was mild—and whacked at the old stump with my dull axe. If I *were* to do this every day all winter I would wear the stump with shocks and scrapes if nothing else—believing as I do that my accomplishments are more like erosion. I might produce something of moment if I lived to be a thousand years. The weather does a lot, too. But maybe I will sharpen the axe, though I have no confidence I can do it well. The compost heap is quite a pile of garbage, which on warmish days is a little ripe to smell close up. Obviously I will have to smother it with soil and/ or sphagnum moss or lime when spring comes on. Will I be able to move fast enough when spring comes not to outrage Nancy and the neighbours? Will I be able to clear and devote a full day to anything—on any one of my projects? Will I have the strength, persistence or interest to carry through 1. garden work 2. photography + printing 3. sketching with my viewfinder, scribble drawings in my Masonite notebook scrap-paper book. Tonight Ernie, Angela and Nancy went to a movie, walking to

the cinema through the snow while I did dishes and listened to Ernie's Philip Glass tapes and some of my own—the Andean music one, especially. It is a good idea, I think, to devote a whole day to one thing—something I do not believe I have done for years, so addicted I am to the bit of this and bit of that approach. Contemporary music distorts (dehumanizes the human voice). Instruments are fine—they are machinery all, even the pan pipes, which are breathy, but push buttons, keys, strings are all mouth and finger-end things. Rock singers, opera singers strain the human voice—a try to give an outer edge of what we know as human. What do I want? Bing Crosby? The mellow relaxed voice prevailed at a time when the hysterical oratorical voice of Hitler brought extremes in intention to the voice that would reach the farthest corners of space.

Monday, January 9

For whatever reason I was wakeful and from 2–4 a.m. I read a remarkable chapter in Mann's *Doctor Faustus*—Zeitblom's memory of Wendell Kretschmar the marvellous Pennsylvania German who, ludicrous in his misapplied zeal and stuttering manner, delivers four memorable lectures on music to a sparse unsophisticated audience, the last of which is about the unsophisticated Beissel of Pennsylvania who invented a whole system of music from scratch. What a marvelous chapter, given to us through the humble scribe, protesting his *ordinary* intellect, recalling the handicapped Beethoven in anguished struggling and the unsophisticated Beissel. This being heard by mocking youngsters who are, despite all, touched and educated by it. I read it all aloud to Nancy tonight but had little chance to discuss it with her since the phone rang. Ernie + Angela came back from the French centre, John began a quickie game of Trivial Pursuit and left for his late hockey game. He is home now, asleep in bed, E + A watching *The Magic Flute* and Nancy is in bed. A great storm is promised for tomorrow. Tonight the domestic tranquility and geniality is delicious. Harry Lusher today told me that when he was younger he could scarcely endure the temptation scene of Mann's. How will it strike me? At five o'clock when John came to pick me up at work it was quite light out, and when I got home I chopped at ye olde stump and removed a lumpish big root that I had been hacking at for some time. It is late but I hate to bring so pleasant a day to a close. People around me seem happy and unrestless. I gloat over three days of conservative stump-thwacking.

Wednesday, January 11
Waking today to the storms still going on — schools closed, Ernie excused from work, but the roads opening and the university going on as usual. John + Ernie tore into the shovelling which was done by nine and so my departure on everyone else's holiday was leisurely and pleasant. Today was one of my literature tirades on Williams' "Aux Imagistes" and "Dance Russe." What I said tickled me, anyway. For a good part of the day I swapped sports tales with Rick Trethewey, who is pleasant company. I have just finished smudging blobs of watercolor on paper and blowing it with John's hairdryer. Fun, but so far as I can tell the rivulets will almost always take on the same configurations. They want the subtle directions of shifts, but accept 90° turns only and that only at first. Later they simply reverse direction. The merging and mixing of colors is fun, but muddiness is likely a result. I would like to achieve sure strokes and blends. Is it a problem that I am excited by almost any color, or any mixture of colors? Isn't it about time that I begin to draw. Without a minimum of ability it's foolish, but I would like to do something [other] than flat abstracts and traced magic-lantern pictures. It is almost as if "Danse Russe" were written for me. Is there a "Dance Russe" which makes poems. The idea of the genius (loci genii) of the household — ritual foolishness, necessary vitality, obligatory loneliness, arranging the colors and shapes — the body *and* the world — like eye tricks — What do young people think of such stuff? They will not say. Most students simply act as if they deeply disapprove of me and my antics. How they hunger for the perpetual stern truth-telling Daddy. I rail like this too much. No, once more I did not hack away at my log. The snow is deep,

and when I arrived home supper was almost immediately served. I should, now that the storm is over, tromp through the back yard—make a path. Everything waits under the snow for the time when I make my squares, paths, huts, statues, trellises to grow things, build things, paint things. What I am after is to make even miniscule progress—of any sort so that winter is not merely put-off time. I think about Nancy's paths—cedar logs laid close together and slabs over in the crookedly pattern she has laid out.

Sunday, January 15

At noon Ernie took Angela to the bus to go back to Quebec. The evening saw John, Ernie and Nancy playing an endless game of Baby Boomer Trivial Pursuit while I read Martin Luther for my tutorial and more of *Doctor Faustus*. Nancy read *all* of Dave's novel [manuscript of *Road to the Stilt House* by David Adams Richards], remarking how different it is, but, though she seemed slightly stunned at the new mode, she felt it was another fine work. I read the first five chapters. In my excitement I thought of perceptive comments on his work—comments which now elude me. It has something like the laughter of anarchy—better because, despite social workers, priests etc., who insist on a kind of optimism, there is the laughable in persistent, articulated futility. Nancy calls it black humor and so it is, but Dave's is not the usual black humor, but something special, which it would be good to perceive.

Monday, January 16

I have toyed with the idea of taking the car tomorrow and doing errands—indulgent ones that I put off, like a trip to the art store and the lumber yards. Today we heard from Dave that he sent off the novel to N.Y. with title *Road to the Stilthouse*, which we all like. I read up to about ½ this evening, wallowing in its strangeness of compassion and disjunction. It is dedicated to me—a fact of which I had been aware. Who else but Nancy and Dave are doing things and progressing. Tonight I tried to find who had written *The Somnambulist*—it is with a somewhat silly idea—about [writing] a piece on a daytime sleepwalker. Well, why not write it anyway—and possibly make it a short short. Scene: library; compassionate librarian who protects the poor fellow while she does research on his case. Does she hang a warning sign on him? We shall see. This idea merged further Friday night in the "what kind of movies can we make" discussion. My head is full of unrealizable pictures—streaks of luminous colors and motifs in my head—now with a bit of doubt that I can execute. But why not be persistent. The cost is not great. I see a child's wagon left at an angle on a twilit hillside; the handle angles smartly back—at rest with the poignancy of objects that clearly have been just recently left, like the coffee cups of departed folks at the house. The handle is at a parade-rest, jaunty angle and is lined up with Polaris or a major lighted heavenly object—perhaps even fits into a constellation—an abandoned daytime object is stellified by being left to the lonely displays of the nighttime sky. The lines that people place between the stars needn't stop there but reach to us—so the observing eye may conjoin. Draw a bear in the sky. Why not keep drawing the connection to objects on our poor star.

Tuesday, January 17

"The Sleepwalker" is, or feels as if it is, ready to come to a head, like an irritating pimple. I am close to setting down an opening tonight, but applied gesso to the two boards I am going to use for my sketch outfit and watched television with John. Also browsed in the Taylor Encyclopedia, thinking again of cork trees and kiwis. The dictionary includes no reference to kiwi fruit, so I will try references at work as well as look up sleepwalking. It is time for a stolen hour or so at the library if I can manage it. Dave came by to see how I was liking *Road to the Stilt House*. Happy was I that I could say I did. I told him that he made me laugh, and then feel like a bastard for doing so. I seek tranquility also for finishing the book. We watched the American Playhouse version of Philip Roth's *Ghost Writer*, an absorbing hour and a half.

The kind of things that makes one want to write, even as Dave's book produces the same result. Ernie came from his class enthusiastic with some sense of accomplishment.

Thursday, January 19

I could not resist a piece in *The New Yorker* about a book-burning incident in Baileyville, Me., since that is so close to here and we passed through the place last fall. There was an excellent account of the persons involved and the community, and all in all it was the most sensitive account of such things I have seen. There was some explicit description and account of what Washington County is like — the poorest U.S. county north of Appalachia. That all made me think about Washington Co. again. I have been recommending *A Different Kettle of Fish* and this article to everyone I meet. Ernie was amused to find me expounding upon fish when he came and sat briefly with us in the SUB [Student Union Building]. I did fiddle around in the morning and listen to the tape I made of *48 Questions* and was invigorated by the *meaning* part of the discussion, which was what set me off before. The suggestion that music meaning is located in the body in such rhythmic and plotted pulses as muscular tension and release, and the connection to the 3 fates. I have not pursued *Doctor Faustus* much further, but it picks up and dies off. I get pretty tired of the tricks Mann plays with Zeitblom, his narrator. This evening [at the McCord Hall workshop] Nancy received praise and helpful suggestions from Rick, Bonnie, Bob. Do I want to want everyone to think as I do? Perhaps not everyone, but every now and then someone. At noon I lectured or rather surprised R. McGraw on how dancing and listening to music probably dispel creative energy. I write because I don't dance.

Friday, January 20

In the evening Nancy went off to Diana Austin's for fiction club and John went off to the movies. Ernie and I listened to tapes and discussed odd musical ideas — some of his imagined inventions and my gleaning things from Mann and *48 Questions*.

I searched through the Radio Guide to see what kinds of things I might want to tape but didn't find too much. I do want to go to the library to see if I can get a library tape of the Beethoven String Quartet which is discussed so fully in *Doctor Faustus*. After a while we watched *Monty Python* and *Late Night America*, where there were three young entrepeneurs who had succeeded in business. 1. pizza delivery. 2. non-fiction videos. 3. importing Norwegian soft drinks. The concepts that emerged were, finding the empty slot (what people want but don't know they want), considerable brass in contacts and selling, and persistence — even risk. My later hours were spent laboriously adding to the short short about sleepwalking. I read some of John Gardner's book about being a novelist—stressing the care and craftsmanship. I am dubious about that for myself and think that when I poke and choose, what comes out is wooden and teachery, but I think I will persist, partly because I would like to see how this story comes out. I would love to write an absorbing short short, though I have doubts that I could do so. Is it true, even at my age, that near-heroic self-confidence can produce value? What a question for someone who loves tranquility!

Saturday, January 21

Bitter cold minus 20–25 F, yet all the same I did chop some of the old stump — taking out compost garbage got me out of the house, and since the sun was shining, a short while wasn't terribly punishing. Another smallish protruberance was separated and fell into the deep snow. From the window the thing looks much reduced, though that is something of an illusion because of the angle. The kiwis look pretty much as they did as they were placed upon transplanting, but they look perky. One of my Masonite sketchbook covers I used for a surface on which to place a stunning clipping of dark red pottery from a Chinese magazine. I used several applications of medium and find it looks splendid. In the evening, after a marvellous meal of spaghetti, we went along with John to film society, where a 1947 Japanese film was playing. Nancy and I found it very good. The story of a man and a brother in law who are lured from their village in wartime prosperity (16th cent), one to become wealthy selling property and the other to try to become a samurai; it was a black and white feast to the eye, even in a scratchy print. The farms, the kiln, the city, the ghostly mansion—all filled the small screen with toned detail and broad, energetic acting. Farm buildings, rock-studded roofs with horizontal hewn poles, large barns with raised interior living platforms were memorable—as were close-crowded streets—indicating, I think, the very different spatial dynamics (for drama, and possibility for human interactions) in ancient places. The horseman abreast in a cramped street loom in a way that seems like a dominating intrusion in one's own living space. I picked away at the Sleepwalker's story and retired early. I just about finished Dave's novel and became impressed all over again. Early in the day Nancy found my jelly notebook in the basement. The discovery inspired future plans to return to jam making. Past pleasures were recalled—Ernie + Andrew gobbling up one jar less than a day after I made it.

Monday, January 23

So here is Monday, another cold day, though the intensity of it is not so great. The Monday routine was usual and my lunch hour and reading of Mann was interrupted by a book salesman and a student. Curious how bland and static parts of [Mann's] work are. I am getting ready for another dazzler, but perhaps it is not coming. Treatment of Leverkun's 12-tone scale does not mean a whole lot to me, though I understand something of it in an abstract way: the search for discipline without reversion to old modes and means—almost a chance/math way of checking the exhaustion of the freedom [route?]. What does this mean about creation in general? A kind of Hobbesian necessity for order at the price of commitment to a meaningless order? At seven I went to Bob's [Robert Gibbs's] creative writing class and read my poems and spouted opinions. I picked ones that could together have constituted a kind of ars poetica and Bob kindly put in his two cents. I have got to the point where I am highly conscious of what obsessions emerge in my poems. Excess and a headlong riding on an excuse for it. John came back from a victorious hockey game with a puck lump on his leg. I forgot to mention that yesterday Mother called. Among other things she reported that Jennifer Clark who must be in grade 1 or 2 was fascinated by *Unsnarling String* and read some of until she had memorized parts. This amazes me.

Tuesday, January 24

A snow flurry that turned into rain and drizzle at night. In the midst of the drizzle tonight Sister Kelly called from St. John and I am to take her courses for the rest of the week because her mother is dying. Earlier in the evening I read the rest of Nancy's novel [*Wise-Ears*] and did so with excitement and enthusiasm. Nancy was surprised that I thought the novel and Dave's were similar in some ways. What made me say it was that both are distillations of what they do best, minus familiar or comforting structures for readers. In both I get intensity, well, maybe distillation is the best work. In both cases I wonder what will happen—what will other readers think. In Dave's the phrase the Seaweed uses—"my family died simultaneously"—is haunting in so many ways, but most poignant is the pride of being a figure in a drama that poor Seaweed has in even using this grotesque wording. This afternoon I spent with Anne Compton and her reading course. After the Tat and Spec [Addison and Steele's *The Tatler* and *The Spectator*] we will read *Pamela* and *Joseph Andrews*. I have been called to come to Tony and Ted's class to talk about *The Country of the Pointed Firs* once more.

Friday, January 27

The snow started around ten, just as Ernie and John came in from playing racquet ball at the French centre. After supper Ernie challenged Nancy's view of Revelations (as devil's advocate) because he is having one of his students read a book on the apocalypse and prophecy. They went at it quite strenuously, and I kept out of it as did John who mocked them from the sidelines.

I have felt all day that my short short isn't bad so far, and I dream ahead to structure and conclusion. It is perhaps silly to have this occupy such a block in mind time, but I am even pleased that it seems important enough to lodge in consciousness so much. It would be good to be jotting other short-short ideas. Well, my seeds came today, which is pretty fast action, and they are already in the cool dark of the crawl space against the coming season. I wrote a letter to Yvonne [Trainer] to go with the packet with my book in it for her. I don't write many informal letters and seemed rusty. I continued with Mann at lunch and find I am coming to a good patch and am approaching the key scene with the devil. Odd enough I have to read Marlowe's D.F. [*Doctor Faustus*] for Arts 100, but not until next week. Art projects seem far away, though not less desirable. I still want to run errands at the art store and at Woolco for cigar box nails.

Saturday, January 28

Weather normally brisk. This work weekend proceeded with continued success, though I am not sure I see the light at the end of the tunnel. From all this day, I think the only interesting thoughts were those welling up from the re-reading of CPF [*The Country of Pointed Firs*], perhaps because I am thinking about what I have to say about it. Starting with the very first section I began to take the being in love with a place seriously with the metaphor of amorous love. Here the book opens into its series of displacements of rejection — all the way from not being part of the community to the ultimate rejection of having to leave this earth — hence the strange business of the waiting place and the aura of death. Marriage is symbolic, chaste and eerie. The allegations of provinciality are scarily valid at the same time that from this rooted strangeness (it takes a stranger to understand the strangeness of a place) it *had been* possible to become like the old sea captains cosmopolitan at the same time as they were local. This is possibly what the passion is for, to marry the now and the afterlife, the spinster woman and the asexual spirit, the rooted hick and cosmopolitan gentile lover of place. All is informed by a kind of idealism, giving through the eye, heart, and sensibility a mystic fusion. Style reflects in that stretches are open and free while the cumulative whole magically (rather than logically) urges through intimations the closing [word indecipherable].

Sunday, January 29

It was a shade warmer outside and I got out to whack another good chunk off the tamarack stump. Some rooty parts came with it and this induced me to bring it inside and carve or whittle away at it. Also I typed sentences for 1013. Now what seems neglected is 1000, but the pieces on Frost await me. This evening for supper—Sunday dinner [two students] came to talk with us about plans maybe to possibly quit the M.A. programme. It is impossible to know what we might have to say that could be of any possible help, so we discussed the bullying tactics of criticism of a structural stripe—women's literature, and writing novels. They took an aloe and left for Durham Bridge at about 11:00 p.m. I know I did miss the puttering and making that makes my hours in the art factory happy ones. On breaks I stroll in the study and look at the plants.

Tuesday, January 31

Written Wed. (I hope I don't forever stay behind). The day of the big storm. 34 cm. by the time it is over. There was some warning of it, but not as much as one might wish. In the morning I took time to go to the downtown library and the art store. It was snowing lightly and felt more like a storm than it was acting like one. I went looking for [a tape of] the Beethoven in Mann, but found it not and came home instead with Schubert quartet 13 and Schumann piano and string quintet and some flute variations. [On campus] I found Conway and we sat until about two discussing among other things his theory of [early] Canadian poetry in which the separated and "sophisticated" poets represent to his mind a writing out to someone, since there were no direct communities who could appreciate what they were saying.

Thus we have *imagined* communities or "others," which may well consist of U.S. or British or idealized readers. By the time Don and I left the SUB it was a near white-out and the university was about to close down. The phones were not working. Around 3:30 I went over to MacLaggan where I found Ernie finishing his teaching and we spent some time with his gang of ELPers [English as a Second Language Program teachers and/or students] pushing students out of the parking lot. By the time we got home the snow was pretty deep, and since everyone was home it was exhilarating and everyone was extremely jolly, myself most of all. I found the wood and gardens book radiantly stimulating. I wished to make nearly every project in the book. After supper I listened to the new tapes while reading my SOJ [Sarah Orne Jewett]. The Schumann flute was *also* exhilarating—perhaps I was hyper! Ernie shovelled out in the continuing blizzard and left after coming in and joining us for goodies before the NHL all star game. How dreary that game was, and all scattered, leaving me to try out burnt umber as an over-marking of charcoal sketching on my gesso board. I watched a silly French movie and fell asleep about 3:15. The storm seemed still going on, but I think it was just blowing around. I could hear the growling of plows and tractors in the night.

Wednesday, February 1

Ern was up—to shovel the Oudemans out—and John was removing a giant plug from out front. I did not lift a shovel and felt very privileged. We heard on the radio about school buses that had not got kids home until 8:00 p.m. What a thing to go through. It was the biggest snowstorm I believe we have had in the last 2 or 3 years. My day was a long one at work, though not particularly onerous, ending in the Ted and Tony seminar, at which I talked too much about my obsessions. One student noted that how often people are compared to trees, which I had not noticed before. Are they more vegetable than animal? I came across several things to look up going through my notes. Nowhere do I have a master list for these odd references and books to read.

I don't know that I have looked up the St. Theresa reference in William James. As I go into the new month I ought to read over what has been written here since Jan. 1, but I can't tonight. I suspect an accumulation of trivia, but also perhaps some kind of chronicle at the least. I surprised myself by writing as long as I have—no doubt I have kept it up because of the expense of this book. What a bunch of $ down the drain if I do not continue. The stump is completely under snow. Even to wade out to uncover it is some kind of task, but I'll get there—at least on the weekend.

Friday, February 3
The Arts 100 lecture was on Palestrina and the telling differences between plainsong of the medieval period and counterpoint. It seems remarkable to me—or remarkably coincidental—that my reading of Mann is dealing with much these same distinctions. In the afternoon I read a fair amount of *Pamela* [for study with Anne Compton] and believe now that I never did read it before. At least I never remember the interests and concerns that I now have as a reader of it. A least I can now read it without the feeling of retreading [sic] the same old stuff.

Saturday, February 4
Warm—up to 50°F and alternating heavy and drizzly rain. When Ern and John got up they went to work getting snow off the roof. Ern too zealous with the axe and yet maybe not. I passed pails of hot water to him out the study window, and he cleared the gutters or most of them on the carport side anyway. The ice hunks clunking through the downspouts made the same noises they had during a thaw at Christmas when Grace got spooked in her room with strange noises. I snoozed in front of the TV while a basketball game was in progress. Later I read *Pamela*. I thought it would not be a good time to write in the journal since the Richardson style could infect what I say—what a foolish thought—yet I have been known to pick up little verbal tics of style like flypaper. As the afternoon passed into evening I began to enjoy the sodden warmth, though I never did get outdoors.

Tuesday, February 7

Seasonably cold -10°C and still bumpy from the ice and snow of Sunday. I spent the morning in the SUB plugging through the last 150 pages of *Pamela* and almost made it. It is, whatever the task, pleasant to drink coffee there and work. For some reason I have always done work better in a coffee shop with people in the middle distance. *Pamela* moved into a comic demeanour that I was unprepared for—the outraged sister of B — yanking on the curtains, Pamela jumping out the window and much sweet virtue rewarded. It amused me to think how much some readers must deplore such stuff. I think I will try to bang out some student writing for my 1013 class tomorrow and rustle up something to say about Margaret Atwood's poetry. Nancy has been typing up film ideas — from an earlier conversation — for Pedersen who told her is going to Berlin to hook up with some promoters. Sounds kind of giddy to me, but she takes my hint that you put as many hooks in the water as you can even if some of them seem extravagant. There is much lottery talk in the office, speaking of hooks in the water.

Wednesday, February 8

Written Friday night, the 10th. This is the first time I've got so far behind, and hence the first time the day is seen in complete retrospect. Was it today that Frederick Prokosch's *The Asiatics* arrived and I plunged into it out of raw curiosity and read nearly a hundred pages, when I should be doing something else? If I recall correctly I spent part of the evening enjoying the curious adventures in *The Asiatics* and then painting while hearing Olympic stuff in the background. I am now squashing thick color on watercolour paper and then flattening it onto Masonite. Sometimes I get a blending of colors that is superior to what I could get with a brush. Two pieces pleased me a bit, a three-color blob that suggested a landscape. So I sketched in a faint trace of a barn bent in the wind. The other was an oval frame of umber, which when squiggled produced a kind of antique frame for a deep blue field and Klee-like squares on top of the blue—the colors fading to seem somewhat lost in and dream-like in the blueness. The amaryllis has two swelling buds and a smaller third one, and the citrus trees look more promising, even the grapefruit which I thought was done for. I want them to hold out until spring when I can repot them and put them outdoors again. They did so well before that I have great hopes for their progress again this summer. How I yearn for a load of soil and several bags of manure. My plans include transplanting the rhubarb and making a box around the hillock where the gourds were last year. Placing the railroad ties to make three beds along the stonewall—and now that I have seen the wood in the garden book, a box and trellis for gourds up against the sunny wall of the house next to the frame—which is now broken down because ice has smashed some of the glass. Another plan is to make duck boards for Nancy's path through the woods.

Thursday, February 10
Nancy's fiction club came to the house to discuss Frisch's *Man in the Holocene*, but I had to leave in order to read poems at the Arts 1000 Cabaret. Their discussion did not seem to be one that I would have enjoyed very much—as far as I could see—because the talk was a lot about relating to characters, and liking and not liking what they had read. Nancy and I discussed this afterwards and agreed that younger people, even bright ones, are much too given to this kind of thing and too little curious as to what is out there and [recognizing] something outside the self. It may be hypocritical of me to feel this about others, since I have got pretty pig-headed about what I want to read and monkey with. Ernie's light went off early. John went to bed, and I went to bed early claiming—somewhat in jest, at least Nancy took it as—that I wanted to get up at 5:00 a.m. to have a magnificent day of accomplishment. Somewhere out there Olympic game action is being watched, though heavy snow keeps falling [in] Sarajevo and events keep being cancelled.

Wednesday, February 15

Warm temperatures and pounding-down rain for a day Nancy says was crowded with incident. It began with gloom when we heard that [a neighbourhood girl] had run away. Between Arts 1000 lecture and 1013 I read poems at Kent Thompson's noontime readings. I gave a half-hour full-tilt. I perhaps scooted away too fast, but I had to get ready for 1013 class and catch my breath. People seemed pleased enough. John called about 4:00 to say that [the lost girl] had been found — to everyone's relief. Nancy had been at [the parents'] house in the afternoon but hadn't heard when she came to pick me up at five, so I was able to tell her the good news. I planned to type my story but my potato basket with my notebook in it was in my office and so I read Raban and thought about projects in my usual moony way. The paper-clip mosaic is a possibility, and images of it fill my mind. There's also a section in the new book I've got on pouring enamel and denatured alcohol onto PVC [word indecipherable]. Something I would like to do but I don't know where I could obtain this PVC stuff. White is pretty essential, I think, and I hope the urethane enamel might be substituted, but who knows. If I make substitutions I'd better do it outdoors for fear of creating fumes. So the list of projects grows and grows.

Introduction to Martin Butler's
Early Recollections

Martin Butler, the one-armed journalist-news-vendor-poet-socialist-itinerant-pedlar-entertainer-temperance-advocate-Canadian-nationalist, needs no introduction to the older residents of Fredericton and rural New Brunswick, many of whom remember him well. A few of these people to this day can recite from memory snatches of his comic doggerel verse.

But in his own time, as well as in ours, Butler's fame seldom travelled farther than the boundaries of New Brunswick and eastern Maine, although for one who travelled this country mostly by foot, crossing and recrossing it — in his peddling days hauling his handcart, "The Canadian Democrat," in summer; and his sleigh, "The Aroostook Rambler," in winter — it was a wide enough world in which to be known. In all probability the readers of his two books of verse, *Maple Leaves and Hemlock Branches* (1889) and *Patriotic and Personal Poems* (n.d.), and of his monthly *Butler's Journal* — which he produced almost single-handedly from 1880 until his death in 1915 — received their copies directly from the author's hand. Butler's writing was choice home-crafted fare to be sold along with his other wares. Moreover, a verse broadside or the latest issue of the *Journal* would often contain self-publicizing portraits of the author-pedlar as an entertaining and harmless character, and possibly would include as well, after the manner of country journalism, some honorifics or comically handled "news" of the customer himself.

Thus in verse Butler celebrated his pedlar's handcart and none too subtly hinted at the kind of welcome he hoped to receive from his rural patrons.

It comes not with the roll of drums
    Or bugle's shrill alarms,
But with a message of goodwill
    Unto Canadian farms

And every gate is open wide
   And every door unbars
Whene'er its banner heaves in sight
   Beneath the evening stars.

Chorus:

Over hill and valley
   Over moor and flat
You can hear the rumble
   Of the Democrat

—and so on for several stanzas.

Butler was born in rural poverty in 1857 in Norton, N.B., and was reared in deep woods poverty, which is not quite the same thing, along the Salmon River. There his father, and indeed the whole family, for women and children toiled as well, endured the punishing life of nineteenth-century woodsworking. After considerable wandering, the remnants of the family found themselves in the Grand Lake Stream, Washington County, Maine, a booming new company town of the Shaw Brothers Tanneries, a place of incredible natural beauty but already in the process of being despoiled by the frantic new industry. Butler's prose, at this date correspondence to the newspapers of Calais, Bangor, St. Stephen, Fredericton and Saint John, describes in full measure the beauty and the squalor, the bustle, wild carousing, gestures of gentility, human aspirations and degradations of life in such a place.

It was in Grand Lake Stream that Butler, who had somewhere picked up early rudiments of formal education, began writing verse and correspondence to the newspapers. Fiercely egalitarian and aspiring to fame after the models of Burns and Whittier —especially the latter—young Butler kept his wits about him by refusing strong drink and trekking a couple of miles to Calais for reading material. It was in Grand Lake Stream as well, on Christmas Eve, 1876, as he was "A-grinding bark on a winter's night," that his arm was cruelly mangled and then severed by the cogs of a peeling machine. After a futile attempt to extract some small compensation from the company, he set out on his perambulatory life....

For a time Butler made his headquarters Grand Lake Stream and dreamed of establishing a newspaper in that "city," but eventually he returned to his native province, where in Fredericton, in 1890, his dream of producing a paper became a reality. Hardly an orthodox periodical in any respect, *Butler's Journal* regaled its readers for 25 years with entertaining accounts of peddling treks through the countryside, with jokes, puzzles and verse, and espoused first nationalism of the Canada-first republican stripe and then later a rather more doctrinaire socialism.

Butler was at his strongest as a writer of autobiography. From his earliest days he wrote little that could not by generous definition be called such, for he was surprisingly and deeply impressed with the significance of his own being and experiences. Unlike other country correspondences to the papers, he always found the dispatches in print over his signature; few events were reported that did not include an account of his part, usually a prominent one, in the action.

Because of his egocentricity, of his naiveté, or perhaps because of his own instincts as a folk-artist, Butler never learned the craft of objective news-reporting—impersonal prose written as if a machine could record and disseminate accounts of third-person events. Perhaps this inability to pretend that his own sensorium did not exist is behind the many contemporary charges that he was a crude and unmannerly fellow. Perhaps, too, his egalitarian sentiments prevented him from considering that his was in any way a being of secondary importance.

At any rate, Butler's irrepressible fascination with the events of his own life is a faith which can carry over to the reader. Surely such a faith is behind the work—however modestly put forward—of any writer of autobiography, though usually worldly station or acclaim is what allows for seemly presentation. Butler's total work, scattered widely in his early years in several newspapers, in his own *Journal*, in his broadside poems, collections of poems, together constitutes a full, minute and lively corpus, comprehensible as a single work of self-portraiture. As a whole, it achieves a seemliness of spirit if not of manner. The selection offered here is but a sample and portion of that whole.

For the samples of Butler's prose selected by Bauer, see Journal of Canadian Fiction *3 (Summer 1973): 181–90.*

Bill Reads: Selected Reviews

The following book reviews by William Bauer appeared in The Fiddlehead *between 1969 to 2002. The earliest of them, like Bauer's first published poetry and other prose, appeared under the name W. A. Bauer, but later his reviews from the 1990s onward had the byline Bill Bauer, as his books never did. From the beginning his* Fiddlehead *commentaries reveal insightfulness, fairness and good humour, along with glimpses of his attitudes to living and his aesthetics. The voices of the reviews are exploratory, questioning, curious (in both senses of the word) and entertainingly lively.*

Except for Bauer's response to Alden Nowlan's White Madness, *the reviews chosen below are abridgements of the originals, with cuts of more than a sentence or two indicated by ellipsis. Bauer also published reviews in* The International Fiction Review, The Cormorant *and* The New Brunswick Reader; *reviews not excerpted here include ones of books by the fiction-writers John Buell, Charles Edward Eaton, Kelly Cooper, Mark Frutkin, Yann Martel and John Updike.*

* * *

Elizabeth Brewster, *Passage of Summer: Selected Poems*
The Fiddlehead 80 (May, June, July 1969)

Elizabeth Brewster is not one of those poets whose reputation rests upon the appearance, every other year or so, of small aggregations of poems brightly packaged and replete with the topical urgencies and modish *ignes fatui* that have developed since the last public airing. Thus it is that her *Passage to Summer*, though identified in half-title as "Selected Poems," will seem to many readers to have the impact of a "Collected Poems." For it is a big book, 132 poems disposed into 12 well-integrated sections, and several of the poems are ones published in her Ryerson chapbooks of 1951, 1954, and 1957. *Passage to Summer* may not be quite Miss Brewster's letter to the world—as nearly as one can predict such things she would appear to be in robust and productive mid-career—but the reader is surely being asked to take her work to date pretty much as a whole.

It is tactical wisdom to make such a request, for the poems do mutually support one another: the whole is more than the sum of the parts. It is agreeable, for instance, to observe that the satirist of "Professor Blake" who moved "a comma here or a colon there" is herself the author of poems invariably impeccable in punctuation and grammar, that the celebrator of apparently simple "truth not afraid to lie" ("Not Poetry, but Life") is upon another occasion having us "Walk opposite / To where truth stands, and you'll bump into it" ("Truth"), that the poet who frequently asserts dismay or at best suspicion of metaphor and childish and adult imaginings does in fact treat such human invention with considerable sympathy as well....

No less than seven poems dealing with her rural New Brunswick past begin with the unmistakable and even insistent "I remember." Poems about dreams likewise usually insist with bold markers that they are dreams indeed—"In her dream," "I dreamed that," etc. Miss Brewster's grammar may be described as one of relentless grammatical rectitude. No slur is intended in calling it that, for she is as boldly willing to play ducks and drakes with rhetorical canons which usually insist upon variety. But she is strikingly the poet of declarative sentences—usually ones that press on, conjunctions located prominently, until syntactical expectations are fulfilled.

> I remember my mother's Aunt Rebecca
> Who remembered very well Confederation
> And what a time of mourning it was.
> She remembered the days before the railway,
> And how when the first train came through
> Everybody got on and visited it,
> Scraping off their shoes first
> So as not to dirty the carriage.
>
> ("Great-Aunt Rebecca")

—and so on through nine more sentences of noticeably similar construction. Such regularity, despite the appearance of the casual, is very far from playing tennis without the net; it is playing the game with the net located obliquely but securely where Elizabeth Brewster wishes to place it. Tedious it may be to talk grammar and syntax, but the poetic woods are full of lesser voices who claim plain-speaking of one sort or another, and some descriptive distinctions seem necessary. Unlike the naïve who think it possible to "tell it like it is," Miss Brewster experimentally supplies each of her pronouns with a clear antecedent. Her poetry contains no slogans.

Should not a poetry so conventional as that of her eighteenth-century manner or so filled with literary echo and allusion as her long poem "Lillooet" or so doggedly rigid in their Ciceronian utterances as the poems discussed above be either stifling or cloying? Or at best old hat? The miracle is they are not. The conventionalities and rigidities produced the very opposite of the comfortable, the self-satisfied, or the reassuring. Like the little New Brunswick country girls pretending to be Queen Victoria or imagining horses to be steeds, there are everywhere in *Passage of Summer* urgent human attempts to transform experience into what allegedly it is not....

To Elizabeth Brewster the game of poetry would seem to be like her game of faith.

> And I remember
> The girl in my office
> Who plays bingo every Tuesday.
> "Some people always win," she says,
> But me—I always lose.
> But I go all the same."

But losing can be winning....

One hesitates to praise a book of poems by setting it against the mindlessness of the present moment, but these like all times are perilous and, besides, *Passage to Summer* provides no slick antidotes to anything. It is too pompous to call this collection a letter to the world: pomposity should be thrown away and letters not. *Passage to Summer* is a book of poems, mostly assertions and denials — mostly declarative, strong, and clear, hence illusions — hence of permanent and abiding interest. "Pretend we belong to a civilization, even a dying one."

Philip Marchand, *Just Looking, Thank You*
The Fiddlehead 113 (Spring 1977)

A weak winter sun filters through the mud-spattered picture window of the CMHC bungalow — 18 thou when it was new; remember those days? There's just light enough here to see Philip Marchand's *Just Looking, Thank You* on the coffee table, the one with all those groove marks the bulldog chewed into it when he was a pup. And there's P.M. on the mint-fresh wrapper of the book. His beard looks like a pile of vermicelli, and the shadow lines are done with hundreds of dots that remind you of blackheads, but the main thing is that he looks inscrutable. Do you know why? It's because he's wearing shades, and — well, when somebody wears shades you can't exactly see their eyes. Instead, you can see these tiny reflections of figures — people dancing, people in a restaurant, and it strikes you right away that you can't see Marchand's eyes; but you *can* see what it is that *he* is seeing. It's a bit spooky here in the half-light. What does Marchand see and what does he think? His half-title says, *An Amused Observer's View of Canadian Lifestyles*. Amused is he?

In comes my thirteen-year-old, Grace, from her expensive ballet lessons, and she spots him immediately, even before she changes into her $20 Levis and applies a fresh coat of raspberry Lipsmackers.

"There's Philip Marchand. What are you doing with Philip Marchand?"

"What do you know about Philip Marchand?"

"Well, Philip Marchand just thinks he's so intellectual, that's all."

"How do you know that?"

"He's in my magazines and he thinks he's so intellectual."

Because we are one of those togetherness families threatening to be untogethered by galloping adolescence and I keep trying to snatch any binding ends I can, we two are soon looking through pages of teengirl magazines. Sure enough, in amongst the ads for acne cures and articles on kid suicides, there is Marchand, going on about movie stars and such things. He scarcely seems to be the monster of intellectual egotism I was led to believe.

So that's where Marchand can be found — among other places — down in there amongst the hardsell items where such as Grace and other readers of the slicks may bump into him. He may, then, qualify without question as a true-blue, capital-letter New Journalist living out reportage in that peculiar mix of personalized-depersonalized knowingness that is said to come from legwork and professional word-smithing. His specialty: what Tom Wolfe so insistently reiterates is "the way we live now." His beat: Canada — the "we" here being those of us from Quebec to the Pacific who have bought "lifestyles" that somebody or other has been peddling. His method: Wolfian — scene-by-scene construction, plenty of dialogue, a third-person-particular-character-point-of-view, and above all — very much above all — scads of physical details, of the kind which is thought to be symbolic of people's "status life" — in other words, lots of brand names and lots of awareness of clothing and cosmetics. After all, not everyone knows that Physohex is for zits. Golly, I've always called them hoobs and used Physohex for the dog's sore ears....

[Marchand's] boast is that he listens well, listens to people recount their own personal experiences — the commuter dweller, the gay bar patron, the civil servant, and so on — and finds from what they say that the quality of their lives is far from what the ads promise. Here Marchand is as good as his boast. It is possible, despite the case with which one can pull his leg for his stylistic tics and somewhat shopworn mannerisms, to believe that he does care about victims, that the artful renderings of what he calls "private reality" are wholesome and a superior kind of truth-telling. "That private reality—the reality of what goes on, not only in the heat of the singles bar, for example, but *after* people have left the singles bar and are driving home—was precious to me." This is the Marchand you have to like—at least the one I do....

If it weren't for those shades, P.M. If you weren't quite so "amused." If *Just Looking, Thank You* with its suggestion of consumer wariness didn't make me feel that savvy is something you've got but can't really pass on to us. What are *you* buying? Nothing. C'mon, Phil. You are the one-hundred and fiftieth writer I've seen lately who has dropped the Gucci name and you of all people have to know what's an ad—whether said in irony or not, eh? And what about your publisher who hustles your book by telling us your stuff is "a little...*wicked*" (the three little dots are the publisher's, not mine)? You're a moralist, Phil; are you going to stand still for that? I don't think you should. Your plain old-fashioned compassion for victims of the hucksters is too convincing for me to believe you're willing to remain all that cool—for very long.... Doesn't this question have to be asked: if you want to nail the bastard behind the zit-cure delusion, can you really do it when your stuff is going to appear right next to an ad that just such a damned mountebank has paid for?

These remarks are probably more severe on Marchand than is just, for he is an extremely talented and very readable essayist.... I've gone on like this because I've bought a few "lifestyle" dreams in my time—the fragile sanctuary of the mortgaged bungalow—a dismal second-hand car for trips to music lessons and cubscout meetings. The kiddies are about ready to be moving out into a worldful of hustlers. It has already begun. I can't get them to read Boethius, the New Testament, Thomas Carlyle, you know. But they will, no doubt, be reading Marchand. Is he friend or foe? I'm sufficiently convinced that he is one of the good guys to wish him well. Most of all, though, I wish him independence from his glossy contexts.

Charles and Samuella Shain, *The Maine Reader*
The Fiddlehead 174 (Winter 1993)

On the map, the state of Maine appears to obtrude shame-lessly into Canada, wedging its way between Quebec and New Brunswick—at best a geographical nuisance, at worst looking like a protuberance of manifest destiny that has lost its sense of direction. The history of the boundary, though, is more of a benign comedy than anything else, owing to the fact that the movers and shakers of North America never lavished very much attention, nor even a little for very long, on this territory. The northern half of this northeastern nose of the Great Republic is still sparsely, if barely, populated, and the southern more industrialized half even today has the feel of fringe territory in a land where life is quicker and scarier elsewhere. Once part of Acadia, once a detached hunk of Massachusetts, Maine was "the eastern frontier," as Charles E. Clark called it in the title of his excellent history of the region.

But Maine, to Canadians from the eastern sections of this country, is a presence less exotic than it is to many Americans. Hundreds of thousands of Mainers over the years have been and are descendants of Québécois and Acadians within easy travelling distance from those of family and friends who had not emigrated. The old train connection between Montreal and Portland made Old Orchard Beach and surrounding Atlantic shores a mecca for both French- and English-speaking Canadian tourists. In the nineteenth century both Maine and the Maritime Provinces enjoyed a stretch of prosperity and optimistic commercial life in the era of wood, wind and sail; both tend to look back at this time, often romanticizing it excessively—especially in tourist-luring icons and selective-memory family tales. The recent excitement over cross-border shopping refers, of course, to nothing new, only to the rising volume of it as a result of punitive levels of pricing and taxing.

On the literary front it is worth noting that when Marshall Saunders' *Beautiful Joe*, that all-time grand-champion weepy dog novel set in Canada, had to be reset in the U.S.A. by command of market-wise American publishers, Saunders selected Maine. Apparently this was no idle choice on her part, for subsequently she wrote adult novels set in the state, in one memorable instance placing her orphan-girl heroine overnight at the lavishly-described railroad hotel in McAdam awaiting the morning train that would take her to her queer, religious foster parents over the line. Then, too, there is the interesting reciprocity in the work of those two giants of historical fiction, Kenneth Roberts of Maine, Thomas Raddall of Nova Scotia: Roberts writing with sympathy and depth of Loyalist characters, Raddall doing likewise at times for Yankees....

Yet the border is a border, and the most striking feature of it is in the change in spoken English that is immediately evident to anyone with ears. The vowel sounds, dropped r's, the pitch, the lilt, and even the ways of fooling are different. What Canadians sometimes do not realize is that travelers from the south and west coming into the state experience this same sudden change. To them, Americans from away, Maine is exotic, strange in most ways, and the sound of the language to them is only one manifestation of the oddity of the place—"And to think it is so near Boston and New York!"

The Maine Reader is but the most recent of many publications over the years that have explored the distinctiveness of Maine as an idea, a quality of mind, a place of refuge, and, under some treatments, full of stuff insufferably quaint to the point of irreality. Charles and Samuella Shain in their anthology have managed to avoid the worst of this dream-place-for-other-folks kind of writing in their selection of pieces by early explorers through to contemporary poets—but not entirely....

The Shaines draw, somewhat sparingly, from those who command inclusion by reason of their stature: natives Longfellow, Robinson, Jewett, Millay, and non-natives Hawthorne, Thoreau, Stowe, and E. B. White. Anthologies do cramp major writers, and inclusiveness is a worthy aim, but this one allots a quarter again more lines to Marsden Hartley's poetry—"Lewiston is a Pleasant Place" is simply a dreadful poem—than to E. A. Robinson. This is a quirky judgment, if not an irresponsible one, despite Hartley's place as a significant American painter. And, it is unfortunate that once again Sarah Orne Jewett is represented by "The Town Poor," a good enough story but one that reinforces the view of her as a local colourist, on the "mere" side, rather than as she is in many another possible choice, a visionary whose work is unique in style and substance....

The Shains comment on Maine's Franco-Americans and their "steadfast adherence to their language, religion, and cultural identity." Such a characterization would have been unassailable twenty years ago, but as things stand now according to most recent studies, it is an overly sunny view. Nonetheless, writing by and about this significant group in the state is represented by examples by only one writer, A. Poulin Jr., with an autobiographical essay and one poem. Neither from Poulin nor from the Shains may we learn of the variety of writing—mostly in French—that was produced, especially in Biddeford and Lewiston from a good time back. The newspaper *The Messager* in Lewiston, for instance, appeared continuously for over sixty years, and its proprietors and editors and many of its readers, who were offered literary fare as well as the news, could by no stretch of the imagination be thought of as an underclass, as is implied by Poulin of all Québécois in Maine in an undifferentiated lump....

To contrast with the sufficiency of rural-life chronicling, more could surely be found expressing the city life of Maine. It is there, after all, where a populous *real* Maine may be found as well. Once again, nineteenth-and twentieth-century journalists should not be slighted, however much even they themselves may have felt they were writing ephemerally. The fabled city of Norumbega was never found by the explorers, and Sylvester Judd's dream of a transcendental-Unitarian holy city never materialized in Augusta. But those lost dreams were replaced with others, perhaps just as futile and more vulgar, but rising from them came real places, real people.

The Shains may be thanked for giving us at least some pages from the diary of Benjamin Browne Foster, a teen-aged autodidact in the Bangor of the 1840s. He was an omnivorous reader, a store clerk at fourteen casting his critical eye on the citizens of his rowdy, raw city and writing his thoughts in a copybook. His is a refreshing voice, and just as real as can be.

Alden Nowlan, *White Madness*. Ed. Robert Gibbs

The Fiddlehead 194 (Winter 1997)

The American novelist and critic John Updike once wrote about his disappointment in meeting his boyhood idol, James Thurber. How different was the man from what he as a reader had imagined him to be. Updike then went on to relate meetings with other writers, decided, for various reasons including the "constructed-self" idea, that such gaps are inevitable. If there was ever a major writer to give the lie to such a conclusion, it is Alden Nowlan, as his innumerable friends and those who may have met him only once can testify. The Nowlan of the poems, stories and novels seemed to those who knew him very much like Nowlan the friend, the neighbour or the colleague. Yet Nowlan himself wrote of the constructed self often and subtly, as in, for example, *Various Persons Named Kevin O'Brien*, and the poetry collections *I'm a Stranger Here Myself*, *The Mysterious Naked Man* and the playfully ironic *I Might Not Tell Everybody This* (the titles always bear sharp meanings). The difference, I believe, between Nowlan's and Updike's crew of notables is that Alden explored and shared with readers the on-going and never-ending process of self-construction, seeing it as a common human inheritance, and in no way the province of merely the writer, the intellectual, or the emotionally refined.

Thus it is that Robert Gibbs shrewdly placed Nowlan's May 15, 1971 *Telegraph-Journal* column, "He Be the Same

Old Al," as the opening piece in a collection of columns republished from that paper. In it Nowlan confesses to feeling an imposter when he received an honorary degree of doctor of letters: "Imagine me standing there among all those real doctors! That's not false modesty. It's a fact of human nature." The piece very deftly and truly goes on to connect this feeling to the roles, titles and positions we all think about and may happen to acquire from childhood onward through life. This, and the fifty-four pieces collected here under the title *White Madness*, are "the same old Al," which in Alden Nowlan's case is saying a great deal. For these columns written weekly under the pressure of deadlines for a daily newspaper are very much of a piece with Nowlan's early work. They serve to remind us of Nowlan the journalist, prompting us to speculate how much insight he must have derived from the professional journalist's concern with the passing scene, the topical and the timely. The self-confessed newspaper junkie (regularly reading five dailies and eight weekend papers) was saturated with print news, both as producer and as consumer.

The focus on journalist, too, can remind us of how much good writing there is in the papers that simply gets read and then all too soon discarded. True, we clip and save, but in my experience if we saved all we might wish to, our houses would be stuffed full of nothing but newsprint.

Still, if we define literature (perhaps crudely but I think meaningfully) as reading one wishes to keep for rereading, then having a small collection of Nowlan's columns is something to celebrate, though as compiler Gibbs tells us in his excellent introduction, he found at least 300 pieces of Nowlan's from his tenure as columnist from 1968 to his death in 1983 that would have been valuable to put between covers. If we can get to keep the writing we don't want to throw away from our newspaper reading, a priority should be to have other volumes of these lively, distinctive and popular pieces of Nowlan's from the *Telegraph*.

Michael Crummey, *Flesh and Blood* and *Hard Light*
The Fiddlehead 201 (Fall 1999)

....In both of these works, setting—as landscape, climate, and human culture—dominates. In the short stories of *Flesh and Blood* the few scenes not set in Newfoundland provide a temporary feeling of disorientation for the reader, though the characters, surviving as well as anyone else far from home, are by no means clichéd down-the-road pitifuls. Their orientation is to understand themselves via personal memory and point of reference, not as representatives of a cultural group with predictable, shared characteristics. Most of the stories, however, take place at home in Newfoundland in the inland mining town of "Black Road," in recent years greatly abandoned after the closing of the mines. The *Hard Light* volume contains prose pieces and poems which derive, as Crummey explains, from conversations remembered and in some cases recorded. Forthright about his artistry in making use of oral and written sources from the past, Crummey makes it his choice as to how to caste these gleanings: in prose, poetry, lists of catalogues. He is deft and convincing in these choices.

The thirteen stories in *Flesh and Blood* may be described best, perhaps, by what they are not. Here we are very far from short stories of dramatic interaction in brief time schemes with characters that the author asks us to understand as types with predictable, assumed assumptions of conduct and outlook. What another generation would have called "exposition," isolated orienting information from dramatic focus, is, with Crummey, merged and is part and parcel with story. What ordinary people want to know about people from their crucial defining circumstances of birth, parentage, childhood, courtship, marriage, work, and death is also what characters in the stories want to know. Moreover, the main characters consult remembrance to probe such circumstances of their own experience in order to understand themselves in the here and now. Happily, we have no authorial nudging of readers to yield to facile, boxed explanations—sociological or psychological—

of which the characters themselves are unaware. We stand with these people, and understand the common humanity of their trials, or if we cannot, we cannot read Crummey's stories with any understanding or affection at all. His people exist amidst the perplexities of their various fates, as do we all. Their determinants accrue over a life-time....

One of the attributes of Crummey's prose in these stories is his abundant use of simile and similitudes. Both the characters and the authorial voice are forever seeking likenesses—often for feelings that are difficult to express. For stories that are devoid of symbol and metaphor with their attendant airs of authorial control and completed definition, the similes with their explicit use of "like" or "as if" yield a more provisional and appropriate articulation. Author and characters share the more modest effort to connect. "I said it was 'like.' I didn't say it 'was'" bespeaks an ongoing assumption that knowing, connecting are, indeed, but provisional. Thus the full range of such efforts from Angus's self-pitying complete that the woman "was as cold as an outhouse seat in the dead of winter" to the authorial description of Austin's response to Melinda's not asking questions about a previous lover: "He felt them, the way an animal can sense rain in the air hours before it arrives."

Crummey's remarkable collection *Hard Light* extends the probing into what is shared and what is individually "understood," as he faces the intellectual and emotional problems of connecting to the past. Shunning the despair of absolutists who wallow in the absence of utter assurances, Crummey has listened to family tales, read documents and memoirs, knowing full well their limitations, but finding in them, nonetheless, the light of life. Free to edit, invent, rephrase and arrange, he produces little prose "stories," poems and commentary. A reader of *Hard Light* might be well advised to begin with Crummey's "A Note on the Text" at the end of the book where he modestly and frankly acknowledges his methods and sources, all the while maintaining the value of the writer's considerable fictionalizing. After all, Crummey has been the recipient of tales told of him and in the past. What is he to do with this heritage—merely be a recipient conduit and transcribe? Others have done that kind of thing. Crummey has more to offer.

An example from the section "Discovering Darkness" will have to suffice. Of this section Crummey writes, "'Discovering Darkness' was inspired by *On the High Seas*, the diary of Captain John Froude (1863–1939)." Froude was fisherman, sealer, miner and sailor who travelled the globe on tall ships and steamers. "The titles of all the poems are taken directly from the diary," as are sections of the poems. Crudely put, the method could be described as monkeying around with found poems, although in practice and result such coarse description would be unfair to the point of inaccuracy. The poem "The Names of the Ropes (1887)" lists the ropes a sailor must know in a catalogue of nearly thirty of them—a poem, as presented, found or otherwise. What follows concludes the poem:

> Which is not to mention the standing rigging
> on which the sailors move along the ropes
> in all weather and sometimes appear
> to be spiders mending a web, while at others
> they appear to be caught and helpless as flies
> in a web of someone else's design

One might wonder which parts of the poem are in the words of Froude and which in Crummey's, but clearly Crummey, by not providing the apparatus for that information, tells us it does not matter. Instead, we must regard the joint authorship as collaboration, one that spans time but joins the generations. That *Hard Light*, a book of 125 pages, is entirely made up of such collaborations makes the book a treasure.

Maureen Hull, *Righteous Living*

The Fiddlehead 206 (Winter 2000)

Maureen Hull is a quilter. We know that from the slight bio-graphical material included in her book of short stories, *Righteous Living*. Moreover the cover of this volume reproduces detail from a quilt entitled "Journeys," by one Katherine Hull…. In one passage [the author] refers to a "Grandmother's Choice" quilt which her character, Ceely, has made. It is untypical of Ceely's other work, but serves, in making and response, as a tribute to her own grandmother, her tutor in quilt making and the only human being who appears to have treated her decently. Consider, if you are tempted to consider this as a lapse into sentimentality: Ceely, who had no choices in her life, at all, carries her quilts to safety from her burning house rather than awakening her three loutish, middle-aged, booze-befuddled sons from their beds. What a moment for her to choose to have them begin looking after themselves!

Less traditional is the other quilting work of Ceely of "Ceely's Choice," but open to understandable meaning in another way. "Her colours seemed to explore from the centre, tumbling over one another in a rush for freedom. Only the firm dark borders she placed around the edges kept the colours from flinging themselves off the quilt altogether." It is clear enough that those dark borders are pretty important, holding off infanticide for fifty years, for instance, until the roasted victims have thoroughly deserved their fate.

Hull's mordant humour, often used in a context of female oppression, emerges as a sign of unsurpressable intelligence or wry internal expressiveness. While Ceely rejects appliqué work, saying she "couldn't draw a simple petal shape on paper," the protagonist of "Leap Year," a mall-haunter who makes what she can of her confined experience, attempts, with the help of the *Reader's Digest*'s "It Pays to Enrich Your Word Power," to write a daily journal (it somehow helps to describe yourself as "impecunious" rather than "poor"). She tells of picking up a quilting magazine from a rack at Shoppers and observes, "I definitely prefer appliqué to patchwork; who'd buy a bunch of fabric, then chop it up into tiny squares, then sew it all back together again? Sounds like a make-work project to me."

Although twelve of the thirteen stories in the collection have female protagonists, they are unlike—as suggested above—in age, experience, and preferences. Some are rendered in first person, others not. What these characters share is limited scope for lives, their choices under the circumstances making them vulnerable to manipulation by others and sometimes brutality, from men, from mothers, from poverty, from their own stubbornness, and so on. But above all they are neither stupid nor unaware. Their talk and internal perceptions are sharp, pithy and fun to come across in a text—so much good wisecracking in story after story! These women's words and thoughts are most often astute enough to perceive complexity and paradox, even when the resulting comedy is self-deprecating, which it frequently is. There is little wholesale villainizing, though heavens knows there are sufficient candidates to loathe or deplore. Interesting, in two stories which focus upon men, it is they who silently suffer domination by their mates....

These stories show rare talent and unobtrusive craftsmanship. Hull is lightning fast at establishing setting and characters and getting narrative underway. There is a deft portrayal of interior life with its hops, skips and non-sequitors, but in this she does not lose the reader's orientation. Though there is a tendency by some to deplore such mental processes as dissonance to be "corrected," Hull's comic vision is built on the emergence of new and expressive meanings from such juxtapositions and from unstructured thoughts and relaxed gab with others. The comic vision (call it "low seriousness," eschewing the "high" variety) is that which tells us best what we are as human beings. Hull's *Righteous Living*, all heart with little or no jabs from a writerly satirical stance, is a good example of just that, and it is not often done as well as it is in this collection of stories. They are highly enjoyable and, if you chose to stop, now or later in recollection and reflect on them, they are admirable.

Bill Gaston, *The Good Body*

The Fiddlehead 208 (Summer 2001)

This remarkable novel triumphantly escapes the market-driver classifications of fictional works so common these days. It is by no means a sports novel, and academic spoof, nor merely a heart-rending chronicle of a man with a wasting disease. Nor is it even partly those types, each plotted to jostle ironically against the other. Yet a simple synopsis might suggest otherwise — might suggest a novel running in some well-worn grooves.

Boddy Bonaduce, after many frustrating attempts as a minor-league hockey player, is diagnosed with MS, prompting him to return to Fredericton where, as a much younger and more hopeful defenseman with the AHL Express, he had married and fathered a son. Having abandoned his family as he moved from one lesser American city to another over the years, his diagnosis faced him with homecoming urges nearly impossible to satisfy. Leah, his wife, was settled in with a mate, a lawyer named Oscar Devries, and his son Jason, whom he barely knew, was private and uncommunicative. Driven by longing, Bobby conceives a plan: to enrol as a graduate student in a creative writing program at UNB (he plagiarizes poems for his admission portfolio), and then to join the university varsity hockey team so that he can play alongside Jason who is, by the way, no chip off the old block on the ice. Bobby's adventures as he tries to carry out this oddly conceived plan are comic and poignant, but are subsumed under the overarching fact of his advancing bodily decline.

Ingenious as this plot is, it is, frankly, possible to imagine it as a mere tragicomic progression of events in the hands of the average contemporary novelist, who without consciously meaning to, caters to readers' expectations, especially in the territory of "knowing" attitude and tone. Where Gaston excels, by way of contrast, is in the masterful creation of his main character, Bobby. Here is an invented "someone" to arrest attention and lodge in the memory—a compelling possible person. The novel might legitimately have been titled *Bonaduce*.

Much of the success of the portrayal of Bobby comes about because of Gaston's choice to make the content of his character's consciousness utterly dominate. What Bobby thinks and what he feels—the rhythms, nuances, patterns and ongoing consciousness from minor frustrations to the onset of physical decline and the looming of a possible early death are everywhere. We hear what Bobby says and what other people say, but almost always dialogue is succeeded by Bobby's take on it. Just as we all do, Bonaduce remembers and plans. Whether we trust his memory and are shocked by his plans or not, we are there. Such intimacy with the main character has immense payoff. In no cute way, but in a plausible one, his professional and passionate life as an athlete in a lightning-swift team sport is repeated off the ice in a mental ever-changing mix of the planned and the improvised. Failures are sudden, and there can sometimes be swift recoveries. But failures can also be irreversible. As Bobby muses to himself about the callow ironies of his young seminar mates, "Those types were magnanimous enough to enjoy the little thrill of a perception broken. But, hey, he'd show them; he could be stupid in ways they'd never dreamed of."…

Gaston's title, *The Good Body*, cannot be taken literally, or at least not entirely so. After all, we are taken through the experience of a man in the process of losing control of his body. Lapses of feeling and uses, small at first, but accelerating, are with us throughout. But it is a good body that is departing. As a veteran of many hockey seasons, Bonaduce has habitually sloughed off pain and injury, learning how to "play through," and relying on his body to heal. Thus his failure to feel panic at numbness and diminishing dexterity: "It wasn't exactly a limp he was suddenly into, but he had to use the handrail and he had to laugh at the timing of how our bodies hate us. Pimples on the night of the date." The body and the mind are for Gaston not strictly continuous, but very nearly so. The novel is full of mind play, but there is constantly what we may call "bodily presence," and it is in play even as the mind is likewise.

Surely something ought to be said about the wonderful texts of Bobby's efforts at creative writing, the masterful scene of Bobby and Jason's presence together at the Bob Dylan concert, the dynamics of the young group of bargain hunter renters which Bobby joins, his gut-reaction dislike of trendy but vapid lit-crit talk from fellow graduate students, his tender relationship with Margaret, his amateur guitar playing and his tastes in music, his nights on the town, and his once-only intense sexual reunion with Leah.

Good body, good mind ever outside the box. Good novel. No, excellent. One of the best.

Kent Thompson, *Getting Out of Town by Book & Bike*
The Fiddlehead 211 (Spring 2002)

This is a rave review, and that has nothing to do with the fact that Kent Thompson was a lively editor of this magazine at one time or that he is a good friend. *Getting Out of Town by Book & Bike*, handsomely produced by Gaspereau Press of Nova Scotia, is a marvel. In 157 pages, Thompson gives us a brief but meaty history of bicycling, discussion of books about bicycling, autobiographical accounts of freedom he experienced with his own first bike, what bicycles mean to characters in notable fiction and nonfiction, the intimacy a rider achieves with the terrain he negotiates, especially if he attempts his own bike maintenance, the real perils facing bikers on today's major highways, and perhaps most absorbing of all, his own experiences biking to the locales important to some of his favourite writers.

It would be tempting to call this work "educational" if that were not a word drenched in connotations of dullness, or seeming to forecast that preachments are forthcoming. After all, no one really needs to be told, over and over, that biking is good for your health and that it is an environmentally friendly pastime. So much is easily implied without the usual hectoring. Instead, Thompson, with his recognizable straight-ahead assertive style, gives us education as going, doing, recollecting, and confirming — or altering — thought. Surprises, new insights are just down the road. There are powerful reasons to go in the first place—and on a vehicle which is, in his felicitous phrase, "powered by human verve." His inquisitive mind is fully engaged wherever he goes, so that the "verve" he speaks of is of mind as well as of body—a mind that recalls what he has done and, more importantly, what he has read in his life before. The boy for whom the first bike was freedom to expand his horizons rides with him still in his mature years. How fortunate he can remember so well, how commonsensical to recapitulate with respect to the memory without having it short-circuited by the dismissive kind of nostalgia that mindlessly devalues the present.

Thompson introduces the "by book" concept of "getting out of town" by the somewhat puckish scheme of riding to small-town libraries and inquiring whether *Anna Karenina* is available to townspeople, exulting when it is and becoming morose when it is not. The "game" fires his recollections of being denied access to the adult section of his own hometown library when he was a boy. Because he believes that the forbidden books held insights and wisdom that were pertinent to the questions and concerns of what he cared about most, he came to revere books, seeing them as capable of expanding horizons, even if in his adult years he came soon to understand that books refined his searching to more questing rather than giving him pat answers.

A novelist, poet and playwright, he learned those lessons soon enough, but as a literary scholar as well—though an unorthodox one — he inverts the *Karenina* scheme and ventures on his bike to locales which were important in the lives of writers he admires. Two of those locales, associated with Ernest Buckler and Elizabeth Bishop, are close at hand to where he lives in Nova Scotia; the other, associated with Isaak Dinesen, is in Denmark.

These jaunts constitute literary pilgrimages, acts which as a type are usually held in fairly low esteem insofar as they are thought to yield anything of value to human knowledge. One thinks of the dough-faced gawkers peeping out of tour-bus windows at the homes of movie stars, [and of] Green Gables, Anne Hathaway's cottage, Hawthorne's Old Manse and the Alcott house. My high-school Latin teacher saved for years to go on a Virgilian tour of the Mediterranean. Little, as far as I know, has been written about this human phenomenon: the desire to go and be in the very locale described in a text or associated in some way with an author whose texts one has read. It matters not a bit whether fact or fiction is involved, and not at all whether or not the crassest kind of commercial motives lies behind the advertising lures set in place. The impulse would appear to be prior to the profitable enterprises that serve such a universal curiosity, to explore the actual or imagined ground of what one has encountered before only as text, to attach significance to locale, hoping for recognition as well as revision of the mental images readers automatically acquire in their armchairs. Thompson gives credit to Richard Holmes's *Footsteps* (1986) for the most probing of inquiries into the whys of such venturing as opposed to the otherwise worthy accounts many literary biographies have written that simply tell us where they went and what they saw. His recommendation is dead right....

Many of the very same people who brought us bicycles subsequently brought us the automobile. Ultimately, the bike, for most of North American, became a plaything for children—with all the freedom-imparting qualities that Thompson eloquently describes, and, sadly, for adults, an almost totally neglected conveyance for practical everyday purposes. But in the last two or three decades there has been a growing number of enthusiasts who for various reasons are on the roads with bikes. It is a sport, and one that brings joy to those who participate. It is almost as elegy for more than one lost life that Thompson recounts the death of a young Nova Scotian who used his bike for everyday commuting to his job. Thompson sincerely grieves the loss of this young man, shares his grief with that of the family, investigates the circumstances of the accident and dedicates the book to his memory.

"But why," asks Thompson, "don't we give up cycling, if it is such a danger?"

"Because it is a joy," is his answer, to which he adds the more easily expressed components of the joyousness. But he also adds the following:

Other parts of the joy of cycling I am not sure I understand. I sometimes suggest that there's something harmonious in riding the spinning wheels on the turning earth in its circuit around the sun, but I can't defend that as anything more than a possibility. It is possible that some of the joy comes from childhood, from the first bike, the first freedom, the sense of flying, the gift of the world. Or something to do with balance; something to do with centrifugal force leaning into corners. Suspended in motion. Upright on speed, powered by human verve.

To which poetry one may only add the words of another poet: "Satisfaction is a lowly thing./How pure a thing is joy" (Marianne Moore)....

Is it not paradoxical that the writer who conceives of great literature as admitting "three o'clock in the morning" thoughts of fear, angst and rejection of happy stuff that will sell is one so eloquent about joy?....

IV. Other Poems

Uncollected

The Launching of the Forest P. Waterman

Little boys in curls and
Sailor suits were there
Clutching their papas' hands
    While the sun smote
    The harbourside and town
With the full weight of noon

And single-galused urchins too
Sat up on the pilings
    Like cormorants and gulls
    And waved their ragged hats
As the proud new beauty moved
Down the ways feeling under

Her the newness of blue water
A Susanna entering her bath
    A band played rich music
    For her and just for her too
A pungent haze of spent powder still hung
Over the cobbles by the custom house

On her decks there trod
Real sailors in actual blues
    Now waving back to all the crowd
    But mostly to the lovely girls
Hoisting sherbet-coloured parasols
To shade their delicate skins

May it not be imagined that
Within this crowd stood the boy
    Longfellow noting the bearded
    Lip of the exotic tar
And learning the public meanings
Of ships in their setting forth

"Where is she bound for?" is the last
Little piping voice we hear from
    The shore; hear in this time
    Who know the fate of the Forest
P. Waterman in her noble age
Alas for the loss of this good ship

Hull up and rotting now on a bar
Where she was tossed from the sea
    Like Neptune's dead puppydog
    Belly to the dry sun
And high tides there sluicing through
Her inverted chambers in all weathers

She is emblem now of nothing we can know
For the poets and the curly-headed lads
    And urchins and girls
    Are dead and gone
Her captains and crews forgotten
All save one whose history now

And name we can record and will
Young Edwin Turley able bodied seaman
    Off the Forest P. Waterman
    Strolled the streets of Boston once
And was seen by a passing artist
He thereby drew the portrait of the sailor lad

We see on every box of Crackerjacks

Beach Scene

There are those who stand on the shores of time
Facing the West and sunset over the sea
And shout *Merde, Merde,* all their days

Merde, Merde, they cry with a kind of elegance
For all their spotted terrycloth beachrobes
And sockless sneakered feet

Oh they are not bronzed statues
Salting from exposure in this air but stand
On the shore of time crying, *Merde, Merde*

Red-rimmed are their eyes from too much sun
Touselled their hair, unkempt their hearts,
Merde, Merde, they cry with a certain elegance

Their voices are birdscattered pipings along the low surf
While oysters suck up pearlstuff out in the bay

Buddy B. Snow

It is a dark hard
Dark bad grievous thing
To be
Buddy B. Snow
Sitting down to his breakfast
In the middle of York County
Gumming his pancakes,
Without the heart
For the riot of daybreak
Or for hoisting the creamer
With the rooster-tail handle
To lighten his coffee.

It is not for you or for me
To tell him otherwise

But for me to tell you
To go slow
If you want to say anything
To Buddy B. Snow.

Carride

This old streetcar I am nightriding
Rackets its way out over
The rim of the earth

Rackets and bangs in confidence
Along the ultimate trestle
While a winking forest of stars
Begins to appear below as well as above

The bulbs inside fizzle and dim
Despite the imperturbable motorman's
Easy stare into his unshelled tunnel ahead
This may merely mean he is dead
His glove affixed to the throttle

We are surely in for it

My scuffed valise is here beside me on the same seat
It is a puppydog God love it he is mine

From an inner pocket next to my heart
I remove a cigar, my last,
Remove as well the band
A scrollwork crimson and gold one
With the cameo half of a woman I think
Flowers of some kind schematic and poignant

I place it on my finger as a child would
Wedding myself to everything back there
Behind us in the dark
My heart is throbbing

O fellow passengers can you not see my heart

It is a giant neon tomato
Lighting up the inside
Of this car

The Death of the Hired Man

The little man mounted
On a stick in the wind
Was made to saw logs—
    Stiffly in a blue gale,
    And with barely a squeak in a zephyr.
However it was that the wind spoke,
He would cleverly go,

Till his jig was up
In a huff too much
And he exploded himself,
    Pins dropping on the shed roof,
    A knobby field of gummed petals
On either side of the ridge pole
Where the wind unanswered blew,

Where his parts flat out
Took the sun and the rougher weather
For a season or two
    And randy clambering cats
    Would give a curious snuff
To his peeling yellow straw hat
Or his peeling red bandana.

The Old Man on a White Bed

Through the whole day long
The old man on the white bed
Dreams

    but not of his sons
    breaking bread with vandals
    three-thousand miles away

    nor of his brother
    and his failed-up sign-painting firm

    nor of his mother
    in her tomb

And the softest touch of
Summer wind bulges the frail white
Curtains of his room

    while he does not think
    of his daughters and their
    moustachioed paramours

    nor of his good wife
    and her healing broth
    even now cooling by his side

But of all the animals
That he never imagined to become
In one long lifetime wasted
As a man

To be ending now as a crook-backed fox
Leaping and jerking above the crusted snow
In fits of pain
His breath in visible staccato puffs of hurt

As an ant uncurled
And curling no more
Floating straight and sideways
Down the stream

From *Unsnarling String*

Ceremony

1 My friends,
    You have been invited here this evening
    To help me celebrate a moment,
    A moment soon to come when I lay
    The last toothpick on the edifice
    Which now awaits disclosure underneath
    The sheet—
        Hello Frank, Edna,
        There are some folding chairs
        In the coat closet over there
        Thank you so much for coming

2 Hippodrome and sports complex entirely of toothpicks and glue
    And has taken sixteen mature birch trees
    With approximately seventy-two gallons of glue
    Oh no, boil it myself on the stove in there
    Whatever questions you would like to ask

3 Yes, even the hinges which allow me
    To open the Southern wall
    For an interior view of where there is
    Sufficient room for three adjacent
    Ice hockey rinks and cantilevered
    Still on the Southern side
    For what we are going to call j'ai lai city

4 Your applause is gratifying
    Although I do not delude myself
    You shine so bright inside as I
    For whom this night is culmination;

And your friendship, I deem, declares itself
All the more because you kindly do not ask
What good it is, but wish me well

For a moment I feel it might be meet
To slit my belly and hurl myself
Across, crushing its delicate vastness —
For you, my friends, for you.

5 I am unashamed of my weeping;
Each one of the little toothpick handles
On each of the 385 toilets, urinals,
And shower fixtures hot and cold
Actually turns
I unashamedly weep for that

6 Art Cooley over here will recall
When I dropped bowling and now will know
It wasn't my back at all, a white lie
— Forgive, like several of you here
Who haven't seen me in church
For a few years now

7 No one will mind, I'm sure
If I ask you not to call it a model,
For it is no copy after anything
Existing on God's green earth
Nor could it be constructed anywhere
Today such would be the cost
The hippodrome proper seating 113,000
People and these dear little wading pools
For tots in the Northeast area
We call Elizabeth and Philip Gardens

8 Modular construction throughout
In that many crucial distances
Are toothpick length or exact

Multiples of toothpick length
The towers inspired by Turkish minarets
Are purely decorative they serve no
Useful function at all
I have avoided symmetry
Wherever possible

9 Approach the table,
Squatting if you have to
So your eye will be the right height,
And see your way in through
The great doors, Gate double E,
And now back into the parking lot for the view
Of the whole of it—waddle if you have to
Not to lose the height of your own wee head—
Look from East to where the West will be behind
And a sun going down
See skyline
See silhouette
And now the banks of lights
Come on in unison
To give us the glowing emerald
In the twilight
I lose speech
I babble of green fields
I have electrified the son-of-a-bitch
For games in the night

10 I have drunk to you for
Your indulgence and you have
Drunk to me for my marvelous folly
None of which matters a damn
To this:
A toast to the contests themselves
Herein to be unwound
From the skein of time:

Horses, men and women, little motorcars,
A million million hotdogs eaten
The size of half a grain of rice,
Victories, defeats, standoffs, stalemates,
Even death perhaps for a mannikin
Pugilist in purple trunks,
But always the fray,
The lighted crowd in from the darkness
Yearning for outcome,
Sundown can happen while
Nobody notices,
O tight wound brightness
Surrounded by my own weak
Piled and daubed glue and little sticks of wood
I have circled you round
And caught whoever will enter
The luminous center:
Let us drink to the game itself

11 Thank you, Clem,
   I'm glad you like it—
   No, I'd be proud to enter it
   In a hobby show,
   But doubt it would stand
   Dismantling and the shocks
   Of transport
   I guess it's like a wine
   That can't be exported
   But has to be drunk
   In its home district

12 The little rushing sound and tiny tapping?
   Yes, I hear it, it's coming from inside
   The Health Club over here on the Grand Concourse
   You know I think that's some poor devil
   Caught in a sauna bath after closing time

No one here that I can see
Has fingers small enough
To reach in there and let him out
So I guess he'll just have to wait
And spend the night

13 Yes, I worry about fire —
And yet I made it
Highly flammable
Didn't I?

Singing a Song Who Cares

Singing a song who cares what it is
At nightfall is the time
For such singing probably alone
But who cares coming home in the dusk?
If the juicy red heart of him wants
Music, it is music that will rise
Through the tubes and bellows of the vibrating flesh
Which is at once the swampy instrument and weedy composer,
The fibrous performer and skeleton audience,
Who leaves his measured foot-tracks on the snow
Like notes on a page
And his sounds in the air
Like birds flying off and away
To invisible and unknown roosts
For the night.

The Grave Old Man Writes a Book for Children

This book is for children said the grave old man;
I am writing this book for children.
The grave old man with whiskers of wisdom
Down to his knobby knees still says
He is writing this book for children.
As the numbers of pages grow greater
And weight and bulk grow foolishly huge,
Text and intricate pictures run on
Like rivers of porridge through the streets of a town,
He believes all the more in his running down heart
That the book he writes is for children

      —the deeper, the darker, the wiser
      —the more the tangle, the more the cacophonous
         hush of words, too many for little heads,
         the more the book is for children.

He knows that this book is a bargain, true value,
And will last for 10,000 rainy afternoons
And countless dark nights of fog and snow
Under cozy lamps in the towns where waiting to grow up
Is a plague of the inevitable

      —that it is filled with intricate, alternate pathways
      —that it has pages and pages of hidden animals
         and animals hidden behind those hidden animals
         among leaves that merely look like pictures
         of leaves with their stems and veins and
         lobes and jaggedy points.

      —that there are forests within forests
         where lost little children who look like
         all the individual little children
         of all the races and nations
         connect the dots within oceans of stars
         into infinite constellations:

> The dragon, the potty-chair, the mailman,
> the lion, the toothbrush, the billygoat,
> the nameless uncle, the fire engine, the cocoa mug

The more the steamy jungle, the polar ice-cap
The spaceship, the lonesome popcorn machine
waiting in the lobby for red little eager mouths
the tumbling, flowery buttery babies
The more the book is for children

> —who will cheer that the book is endless
> that the author is a grave old man
> who can never stop writing the book
> which will leave them with more unread words.
> when they themselves are grave old men and woman
> than dreaming the impossible itself could do

The grave old man has done this
And he goes on doing it
knowing the piled up
cast-off
spilled and neglected
barren and negligible
unread seeds
that are back there
waiting to grow

And also the blank white leaves, left so;
where the children can draw with their crayons
are never filled up with smoky chimneys enough
nor spidery suns with crooked sunrays
to color and settle
the infinite universes there
in the doomsday book for children.

by the grave old man
who is writing his book for children.

From Projects and Contemplations

The seams are bleeding their mortar and
Close to our attention.
Hurrah for the edifice
Nonetheless.

The secret of his animus
Is revealed.

                        Theophilus Washburne

Consider
A treasure chest
Rusty-hasped in a far field
Where the indifferent weathers
Climb up and down
Its bulging sides

That could be the day
To wander
In the lost woods

           *   *   *

The world is a thumbed volume
Fleecy thick
With the unheard words of God

Turn a few pages
Before breakfast on a second Tuesday

So what if you return to hens' eggs
Snapping in the common grease

Wasn't that the menu
Anyway?

           *   *   *

Consider a windowless stone tower
In a dense wood

Consider the inside
Of the inside of it

Though it may be irrelevant
Picture the millions of yellow leaves
Sifting to the forest floor

And then the snows coming
Filling everything up
All around

Consider the possibility that there may be
Something in there
Way inside

In the dead of winter

Like a BB
In a vat of grease

*　*　*

Tell
The first person who asks you
How you are

That you feel
Like the shadow of a rush
Bending before
The onslaught of vacuum
Under a belljar

Or like a universal
Crimson ladybug
Flying home to her children
In the blurred dream
Of the screw-wormed moose

Think of more and bury
Every inquiry
Under a tone of
Nuance

*　*　*

Concentrate on the plausible
Do not waste the day
Hoping that an uncle
You've never heard of
Will send you a
Little monkey in a velvet suit
From an exotic land
Nor squander time in a quandary
As to whether a rhesus can
Be toilet trained
Or how much the cleaning bills
Are likely to be
For a simian Fauntleroy suit
Sent out a dozen times a week
But instead you may
In the push and pull
Of daily doing and doing this day
Hope that tonight
There won't be Shepherd's pie
For supper

*　*　*

Become a manager
Or an overseer
Or at least a foreman
Even if you have to volunteer
For charity work to achieve such a position
Get the reins in your hands for a while
Get an expense account
Get the swing in your step that follows from same

Get the giggle in your diaphragm
That comes for not abusing the power that you have
Let your fingers graze over the action buttons
Without pushing them
Feeling the extended orgasmic thrill
Of bossman interruptus

*   *   *

Imagine around yourself
A proscenium arch
Act as if it were really there
Always
Be aware of profile
And sitting down gracefully
Collapsing the back leg first
Groom the back of your head
And shine the heels and soles of your shoes

Before you turn around
Or tumble upside down
You will suddenly hear applause
Damned if you won't

It may be stupid
For such a thing to happen
It may be unfair
But you may bet your spiritual equity membership
That is exactly what
Will take place

*   *   *

Today it would be good to opine
Something that is to say
To deem it
A good day for deeming
It wise or unwise

Do not merely rake the leaves
With simple unreflected-upon
Sweeps of the spring-tined lawnrake

No

Instead of that
Deem it wise to do so

And do it
Thatway

* * *

There are some mornings
That feel windswept
Though the dark night of sleep
Has been calm
And everything is in its place
Say as the sun finds
The trashbarrels
Where they were left the night
Before
And the lawnrake leans against the shed

Could you say that the great soft clouds
Have simply hopped out of the sky
Like giant toads

Silently

Overnight

* * *

Be aware that when you can remember
To think of it
Of the fellow on a distant hill
Or up a tree
His legs clamping a stout branch

Who has his field glasses
Always trained on you
Those black-rimmed lenses
Forever swivelling
In front of his turreting head
In order to scan you even more
He is so faithful and relentless
He must be in the employ
Of a tyrannous foreign government
Whose ideology keeps him fanatically awake
And vigilant
It is true that the enemy never sleeps
Or to put it another way
What never sleeps
By definition
Is the enemy

From Unsnarling String

I

i   I am making it worse
than it was
before

ii   First is to get ahold
of the ends of you
of which there appears
to be none,
or only one,
or three

iii   Within your massive
unimaginable ramified
major whorls
are a thousand buried grannies
bowlines and sheepshanks
who got born
like unwelcome tumbling
monkeys in daydreams

iv   For the purposes of mental health
it is necessary to see some
progress, every once in a while,
however tiny

v   The ethics of a quitter
are devious
a tangle themselves
and born of the
challenge itself
one is seldom pleased
with oneself

vi   Why are you doing this?
For the God-damned fun of it
can't you tell?

213

vii If you were spaghetti
     your complications would come to
     naught, in paste,
     your networks masticated
     to simple nutriment

viii This must be what the inside
     of the brain looks like
     when it doesn't feel good
     pathways known only to itself,
     but not really

ix   Somewhere beyond the sunset
     is something long and flat
     and ready for the spool,
     or the ball, for winding
     on and
     off

x   I am making it worse
     than it was before

III

I am Laocoon struggling with my garden hose
Which has me hog-tied in the yard.
My father, visiting,
Solves the knots and sets me free.
"How do you do that so easily," I ask him
And he says, "You could too if you were
Forty years in the hardware business."
It is a kindly thing for him to say
But I know as I gaze
At the long, harmless green snake in the grass
The reason why it is
I have not been in the hardware business myself
For the past twenty-five.

IV

i   I have found a kind of resin
I can pour over you
And turn you into
a work of art
expressing either the essence
of string (wherein you are allowed to be
yourself) or something rather grand
called modern reality.

v   You are a three-dimensional roadmap
that only fools would try to read,
even though you are the only
honest-to-God true roadmap
of the world we travel
every day.

viii You permanent
pig-pile of stubborn
fibres, have you never
heard of entropy?
disorganize yourself
like the rest of the universe
is doing.

x   The human race is calling
trillions strong, all to me, in
Babel-voiced unison:
"Here, let me give it a try.
you don't seem to be getting
anywhere."

V

i   Says the left-hand side of the brain
to the right-hand side of the same
(they have never got along very well together)
"if you would shut up for a minute,
we might get somewhere."

vi "Aren't you ever coming to bed?"
     "No, never again."
     "What are you doing down there
     in the kitchen at this hour?"
     "Having the time of my life
     failing to unsnarl string."

vii "It gives me great pleasure
     to present the Stringfellow Barr
     Award for the person whose
     fingers most resemble pieces
     of spongecake or railroad spikes."

viii Snarled string has beady eyes
     and a curly tail
     ever so long.

x   As we learn from the old novels
     at one time a gentleman never had
     to unsnarl his own string
     but had a servant
     to do it for him
     which explains how certain
     cheerful views of life
     made such great
     headway once and now
     no longer prevail.

VI

vi *Rest in peace*
     the tombstone says
     his life was one of
     exemplary harmlessness
     because he fooled it away
     trying to unsnarl string
     that anyone else could have handled
     in five minutes.

vii If there were but only
     three like me in the world
     we could join forces
     and be
     an unsnarling string quartet.

ix "And what are you going to do
with it once you have it
unsnarled?" the philosopher
says, pompously thinking thereby
that trying to
answer that one I will
have to leave it alone
because I had never
thought of such a
fundamental question before.
"I will then have string,"
I tell him wearily,
"as it was meant to be
and once unsnarled
it will be entirely
ready to use."

VIII

i I saw the dawn come
over the hill
a string at a time

vii As the world judges matters
my little snarled string
does not add up to much
as a problem.
I know that
I haven't lost my
sense of perspective on a global basis
whatever appearances may suggest
but also as the world judges things
anyone who couldn't
unsnarl what I've got here before me
can't amount to very much
either.

viii I inherited this snarled string
     from my mother
     who inherited it from her father
     whose father brought it
     over from the old country
     —or did I just dream that?
     My mother claims it is
     not true so which one of us
     is right?

ix   I notice I sometimes
     say "snarl" when I mean "unsnarl"
     or "unsnarled" when I mean
     "snarled"—do you suppose
     that might carry over to doing
     the job itself and might
     be part of the problem?
     My fingers make the
     same mistake?

x   When I am wound
     in my winding sheet
     I only ask
     to be wound up neat.

X

If every snarl has seven snarls
and each of those snarls has seven more
and each of those in turn has seven
and those seven, seven
and those seven, seven each
how many snarls in all?

Answer: One.

Notes and Acknowledgments

The three stories from the 1979 collection, *A Family Album*, are reprinted with permission of its publisher, Oberon Press. Thanks to the William Bauer estate for agreeing to the publication of all other writings. The chapbooks, *Cornet Music for Plupy Shute* and *Everett Coogler*, were both published by New Brunswick Chapbooks; the collections, *The Terrible Word* and *Unsnarling String*, by Fiddlehead Poetry Books.

Until now the undated poems "Beach Scene" and "The Death of the Hired Man" were only in manuscript. Others in this book's "Uncollected Poems" appeared only in journals or anthologies: "Buddy B. Snow" in *The Brunswickan* Jan. 28 1972; "The Launch of the Forest P. Waterman" in both *Ninety Seasons: Modern Poems from the Maritimes*, ed. Robert Cockburn and Robert Gibbs (McClelland & Stewart, 1976) and *The Atlantic Anthology, Vol. 2*, ed. Fred Cogswell (Ragweed, 1985); "The Old Man on a White Bed" in *The Cormorant* (Spring 1989); and "The Carride," in *The Fiddlehead* (Autumn 2010). Three parts of "Projects and Contemplations" reprinted here appeared in the first printing of the poem in *The Fiddlehead* (Fall 1979), but not in the version found three years later in *Unsnarling String*. "Pig-of-the-Wind: Fragments from the Archives" appeared first in *The Fiddlehead* (Jan.–Feb. 1969) and "Never Bet on a Dead Horse" in *The Canadian Fiction Magazine* (Spring 1974), reprinted in *Magic Realism*, ed. Geoff Hancock (Toronto: Aya, 1980).

Of the writings in "Other Prose," Bauer's introduction to Butler's *Early Reminiscences* was in *The Journal of Canadian Fiction* (Summer 1973) and "Wobblings and Warblings" in *The Fiddlehead* (Special issue: *Reflections on a Hill Behind a Town*) (Spring 1980). Sources and dates of the book reviews are included in the text of this reader. "Titles for 25 Familiar Essays," only in manuscript until now, derives from two undated sheets including about 100 titles; the editor has selected and ordered the titles.

Parts of the introduction to this William Bauer reader appeared in a tribute/memoir published in *The Fiddlehead* (Fall 2010). That prose piece concluded with the sentence: "Some of us may soon find ourselves dreaming — okay, I'm already dreaming — of *The William Bauer Omnibus* or *The Bill Bauer Reader*." Poems and a postcard story cited in the introduction but not included in the *Reader* appeared in *The Terrible Word, Unsnarling String* and *Prism* (Fall 1984).

Warm thanks to publisher Keith Helmuth for all the enthusiasm he has shown for this project, as well as his cooperative spirit and his deep dedication to New Brunswick culture. This reader also wouldn't have been possible without Brendan Helmuth's skills and fine eye for printing and book design.

The cover art, by William Bauer, was inspired by his listenings to Glenn Gould's 1981 recording of Bach's *Goldberg Variations*. Thanks to Stephen May for permission to use Bill's piece of art.

Thanks above all to Nancy Bauer for saying yes to an old friend's brainwave to edit a wide-ranging gathering of her dear husband's writing; to Jocelyne Thompson of the Harriet Irving Library, for help in tracking down hard-to-find poems; and to William Bauer for the great gifts of his friendship, original mind and creative practices.

About the Author

William Bauer (1932–2010), born and raised in Maine, completed degrees in Massachusetts, Connecticut, and North Carolina. In 1965 when the University of New Brunswick hired him to teach, he and his writer wife, Nancy, moved to Canada. Over the next thirty years Bauer taught many fields of Literature at UNB, with a specialization in 18th-century British Prose. Also a teacher of Creative Writing, he worked as both Poetry and Fiction editor for *The Fiddlehead*, and—with Nancy, a fiction-writer—belonged to a long-lasting writing workshop known under several names: The Ice House, McCord Hall, Tuesday Night. Bauer published two poetry chapbooks, *Cornet Music for Plupy Shute* and *Everett Coogler*; two full-length collections of poetry, *The Terrible Word* and *Unsnarling String*; and a selection of short stories, *A Family Album*. Much of his family-centred life revolved around his and Nancy's children Ernie, Grace and John. His fascination with creativity in its many forms prompted him to experiment with pursuits such as painting, rug-hooking, papier-mache art, and gourd-painting.

About the Editor

Brian Bartlett, born in 1953 in St. Stephen, NB, has published many collections and chapbooks of poetry, including *The Watchmaker's Table*, *The Afterlife of Trees*, and *Wanting the Day: Selected Poems*. His other publications include two books of nature writing, and a compilation of his prose on poetry. He has also edited many books, including selections of New Brunswick poets Dorothy Roberts and Robert Gibbs, and *Collected Poems of Alden Nowlan*. Bartlett taught English and Creative Writing at Saint Mary's University in Halifax for nearly thirty years before his retirement in 2018.